WORKBOOK

3A
FOCUS
ON
GRAMMAR
AN INTEGRATED SKILLS APPROACH

THIRD EDITION

MARJORIE FUCHS

PEARSON
Longman

FOCUS ON GRAMMAR 3A: An Integrated Skills Approach
Workbook

Pearson Education, 10 Bank Street, White Plains, NY 10606

Staff credits: The people who made up the **Focus on Grammar 3 Workbook** team, representing editorial, production, design, and manufacturing, are listed below: Rhea Banker, Nancy Blodgett, Aerin Csigay, Karen Davy, Christine Edmonds, Nancy Flaggman, Ann France, Laura Le Dréan, and Kathleen Silloway.
Cover images: (center) Harold Sund/Getty Images, (middle) Nick Koudis/Getty Images, (background) Comstock Images/Getty Images
Text composition: ElectraGraphics, Inc.
Text font: 11/13 Sabon, 10/13 Myriad Roman
Illustrator: Susan Scott, pp. 25, 170, 171.
Photo credits: **p. 5** *(left)* Digital Vision/Getty Images, *(right)* Amos Morgan/Getty Images; **p. 15** *(top)* Bettmann/Corbis, *(bottom)* Bettmann/Corbis; **p. 16** Library of Congress; **p. 18** AP/Wide World Photos; **p. 56** Trapper Frank/Corbis Sygma; **p. 78** *(top)* Allsport Photography USA, Inc., *(bottom)* Reuters/Corbis; **p. 92** RubberBall Productions; **p. 95** Hulton Getty; **p. 106** Image Source/Getty Images; **p. 114** Royalty-Free/Corbis; **p. 118** Colin Garratt/Milepost 92^1/$_2$/Corbis; **p. 135** RubberBall Productions.

ISBN: 0-13-189996-1 (Workbook Volume A)

LONGMAN ON THE **WEB**

Longman.com offers online resources for teachers and students. Access our Companion Websites, our online catalog, and our local offices around the world.

Visit us at **longman.com**.

Printed in the United States of America
5 6 7 8 9 10—V001—12 11 10

Contents

PART I: Present, Past, and Future: Review and Expansion

Unit 1 Present Progressive and Simple Present   1
Unit 2 Imperative   9
Unit 3 Simple Past   12
Unit 4 Past Progressive and Simple Past   19
Unit 5 *Used to*   24
Unit 6 Future   27
Unit 7 Future Time Clauses   35
Unit 8 *Wh-* Questions: Subject and Object   39

PART II: Pronouns and Phrasal Verbs

Unit 9 Reflexive and Reciprocal Pronouns   43
Unit 10 Phrasal Verbs   46

PART III: Modals and Similar Expressions

Unit 11 Ability: *Can, Could, Be able to*   51
Unit 12 Permission: *Can, Could, May, Do you mind if*   59
Unit 13 Requests: *Can, Could, Will, Would, Would you mind*   63
Unit 14 Advice: *Should, Ought to, Had better*   68
Unit 15 Suggestions: *Let's, Could, Why don't, Why not, How about*   73

PART IV: Present Perfect

Unit 16 Present Perfect: *Since* and *For*   77
Unit 17 Present Perfect: *Already* and *Yet*   81
Unit 18 Present Perfect: Indefinite Past   85
Unit 19 Present Perfect and Simple Past   89
Unit 20 Present Perfect Progressive and Present Perfect   94

Workbook Answer Key   AK-1

Tests
Units 1–8   T-1
Units 9–10   T-6
Units 11–15   T-8
Units 16–20   T-10

Answer Key for Tests   T-12

About the Author

Marjorie Fuchs has taught ESL at New York City Technical College and LaGuardia Community College of the City University of New York and EFL at the Sprach Studio Lingua Nova in Munich, Germany. She holds a master's degree in Applied English Linguistics and a Certificate in TESOL from the University of Wisconsin–Madison. She has authored and co-authored many widely used books and multimedia materials, notably **Crossroads**, **Top Twenty ESL Word Games: Beginning Vocabulary Development**, **Families: Ten Card Games for Language Learners**, **Focus on Grammar 3** and **4: An Integrated Skills Approach**, **Focus on Grammar 3** and **4 CD-ROM**, **Longman English Interactive 3** and **4**, **Grammar Express Basic**, **Grammar Express Basic CD-ROM**, **Grammar Express Intermediate**, and the workbooks to the **Longman Dictionary of American English**, the **Longman Photo Dictionary**, **The Oxford Picture Dictionary**, **Focus on Grammar 3**, and **Grammar Express Basic**.

Present Progressive and Simple Present

1 | SPELLING

Write the correct forms of the verbs. Make spelling changes where necessary.

	-ing	*-s or -es*
1. do	*doing*	*does*
2. get		
3. give		
4. grab		
5. have		
6. plan		
7. say		
8. start		
9. try		
10. watch		

2 | PRESENT PROGRESSIVE OR SIMPLE PRESENT

Read the sentences about a student, Antonio Lopes. Complete the sentences. Use the present progressive or the simple present form of the verbs in parentheses. Use contractions when possible.

1. It's 8:00 A.M. Antonio Lopes _____*is driving*_____ to school.
   (drive)

2. He _____drives_____ to school every day.
   (drive)

3. The trip usually _____takes_____ 25 minutes.
   (take)

4. Today it 's ___does not take___ 25 minutes.
   (not take)

5. It ___is taking___ much longer.
   (take)

(continued)

1

6. Workers _____ *are repairing* _____ the highway this morning.
   (repair)

7. Because of the construction, Antonio _____ *is useing* _____ Parson Road.
   (use)

8. He _____ *does not* _____ usually _____ *use* _____ Parson Road.
   (not use)

9. Normally, he _____ *takes* _____ Route 93.
   (take)

10. Traffic always _____ *moves* _____ faster on Route 93.
    (move)

11. Today, the weather _____ *slowing down* _____ the traffic too.
    (slow down)

12. It _____ *is raining* _____ hard, and the roads are slippery.
    (rain)

13. Antonio _____ *does not like* _____ to drive in the rain.
    (not like)

14. He always _____ *drives* _____ slowly when the roads are wet.
    (drive)

15. The radio is on, and Antonio _____ *listening* _____ to the traffic report.
    (listen)

16. He always _____ *listening* _____ to the radio on his way to school.
    (listen)

17. The announcer _____ *describing* _____ an accident on Parson Road.
    (describe)

18. Traffic _____ *do not move* _____ because of the accident.
    (not move)

19. Antonio _____ *Hate* _____ to drive when the traffic is bad.
    (hate)

20. He _____ *do not want* _____ to be late for school.
    (not want)

21. He never _____ relaxed when he is behind the wheel.
    (feel)

22. He _____ he can't do anything about the traffic conditions.
    (know)

23. Antonio _____ sorry he didn't take the bus instead!
    (be)

3 | PERSONALIZATION

Complete these statements with information about yourself. Use the present progressive or the simple present.

1. At the moment, _____.

2. I always _____.

3. I never _____.

4. These days _____.

5. I sometimes _____, but now I _____.

4 | PRESENT PROGRESSIVE OR SIMPLE PRESENT

Complete the following postcards with the present progressive or simple present form of the verbs in the boxes. Use contractions when possible.

get	have	look	rain	stand	start	take	~~travel~~

A.

Dear Carlos,

Ana and I ___are traveling___ through England. Right now I
1.
___'m standing___ in front of Big Ben. It's a cloudy day. The sky
2.
_____ darker by the minute. It ___looks___ like it's going to
3.   4.
rain. (It ___rains___ here a lot!) Ana ___has___ her camera, and
5.   6.
she ___is teking___ pictures. Oh, no! It's ___starting___ to rain.
7.   8.

See you in a few weeks!

Marcos

help	improve	live	love	miss	speak	study	want

B.

Dear Amanda,

Here I am in Paris! I ___love___ it here. It's a
1.
beautiful city. I ___study___ French and ___is live___
2.   3.
with a French family—the Michauds. My French ___is improving___ because I
4.
always ___speak___ it "at home."
5.
The Michauds are great. They ___helping___ me find a job. I
6.
___want___ to save enough money to travel in August. Why don't you
7.
come and visit me? I ___miss___ you!
8.

Melissa

5 | AFFIRMATIVE STATEMENTS

Aldo and Emilia Bottero are students. Look at what they do every day. Complete the sentences about their activities. Choose between the present progressive and the simple present.

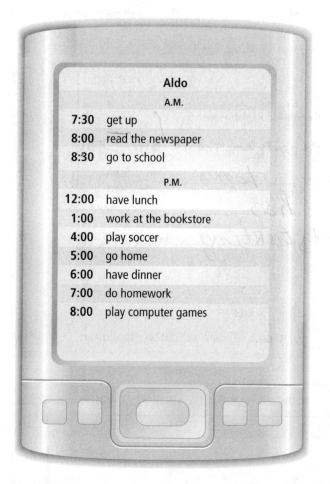

Aldo

A.M.

7:30	get up
8:00	read the newspaper
8:30	go to school

P.M.

12:00	have lunch
1:00	work at the bookstore
4:00	play soccer
5:00	go home
6:00	have dinner
7:00	do homework
8:00	play computer games

Emilia

A.M.

7:30	get up
8:00	run
8:30	go to school

P.M.

12:00	have lunch
1:00	study at the library
4:00	play basketball
5:00	do homework at the library
6:00	practice the guitar
7:00	have dinner
8:00	watch TV

1. At 7:30 A.M., <u>Aldo and Emilia get up.</u>

2. It's 8:00 A.M. <u>Aldo is reading the newspaper. Emilia is running.</u>

3. At 8:30 A.M., _____

4. It's noon. <u>old and Having Lunch</u>

5. At 1:00 P.M., <u>olo and work the bookstor</u>

6. At 4:00 P.M., <u>old play saker and EM is doing.</u>

7. It's 5:00 P.M. <u>old is going Houme and En doing Ho</u>

8. At 6:00 P.M., _____

9. At 7:00 P.M., <u>old does homme work and</u>

10. It's 8:00 P.M. _____

6 | AFFIRMATIVE AND NEGATIVE STATEMENTS

Read this article about Aldo and Emilia from the school newsletter. There are five mistakes in facts about their schedules. Look at their schedules in Exercise 5. Then correct the mistakes.

Modern Language Institute Newsletter

Welcome, New Students!

We are happy to welcome two new students, Aldo and Emilia Bottero from Rome, Italy. The Botteros have a very busy schedule. They both get up at 8:30 every morning. Then Aldo watches TV, and Emilia goes for her morning run. They then leave for the Institute where they are studying English this summer. After three hours of class, they have

lunch together. After lunch, Emilia works at the bookstore. Both students love all types of sports. These days Aldo is playing soccer and Emilia is playing tennis. Emilia also plays the guitar. "We're very happy to be here," they said. "Our days are busy, but we always have dinner together. Just like back home in Italy."

1. _They don't get up at 8:30._

   They get up at 7:30.

2. _____

   _____

3. _____

   _____

4. _____

   _____

5. _____

   _____

7 | QUESTIONS AND SHORT ANSWERS

Use the words in parentheses and the present progressive or simple present to write questions about Aldo and Emilia. Look at their schedules in Exercise 5 and answer the questions.

1. (Aldo and Emilia / go to school)

   A: _Do Aldo and Emilia go to school?_

   B: _Yes, they do._

2. (When / Aldo and Emilia / get up)

   A: do aldo and Emilia get up?

   B: _____

3. (Emilia / walk in the morning)

   A: Does Emilia walk in the morning?

   B: _____

4. It's 12:00. (What / they / do / now)

   A: are they do now? What are they doing now?

   B: _____

5. It's 1:00. (Aldo / do homework now)

   A: Is aldo doing homework now?

   B: _____

6. (Emilia / do her homework at school)

   A: does Emilia do her homework at school?

   B: _____

7. (When / Emilia / play basketball)

   A: when does Emilia play basketball?

   B: _____

8. (Aldo / play computer games before dinner)

   A: Does Aldo play computer games before diner?

   B: _____

8 | ADVERBS AND WORD ORDER

Unscramble the words to make sentences. Use the correct form of the verbs in parentheses.

1. Aldo / the newspaper / (read) / always

   Aldo always reads the newspaper.

2. on time / usually / Emilia / (be)

   Emilia is usually on time.

3. never / school / Aldo and Emilia / (miss)

   Aldo and Emilia never miss school.

4. these days / they / (study) / English

   They study English these day.
   are studying

5. usually / they / Italian / (speak)

   They usually speak Italian.

6. (speak) / English / now / they

   They speak Englis now.
   are speaking

7. (do) / their homework / Aldo and Emilia / always

   Aldo and Emilia always do their homework their.

8. (be) / Aldo / tired / often

   Aldo is often tired. ✓

9. usually / (eat) / the students / in school / lunch

   Students usually eat lunch in the school.

10. hungry / they / (be) / always

    They are always hungry

11. Emilia / at the moment / (have) / a snack

    Emilia goes at the moment a snack.
    is having a snack at the moment.

12. (go) / to bed / rarely / Emilia / late

    Emilia goes rarely to bed late.

9 | EDITING

Read this student's e-mail. There are eleven mistakes in the use of the present progressive or simple present. The first mistake is already corrected. Find and correct ten more.

Hi, Andrew!

How are you? ~~I write~~ *I'm writing* you this e-mail before my class.

I ~~am~~ hav*e*ing a part-time job as a clerk in the mail room of a small company. The pay isn't good, but I'm lik*e*ing the people there. They're all friendly, and we ~~are~~ speak*e*ing Spanish all the time. I'm also tak*e*ing Spanish classes at night at a language institute. The class ~~is~~ *meets* meeting three times a week. It just started last week, so I'm not ~~knowing~~ many of the other students yet. They seem nice, though.

I'm thinking that I'm beginning to get accustomed to living here. At first I experienced some "culture shock." I understand that this is quite normal. But these days I meet more and more people because of my job and my class, so I'm feeling more connected to things.

What do you do these days? Do you still look for a new job?

Please write when you can. I'm always lik*e*ing to hear from you.

Brian

10 | PERSONALIZATION

Write a note to a friend. Tell your friend what you are doing these days.

Imperative

1 | AFFIRMATIVE AND NEGATIVE IMPERATIVES

Write affirmative and negative imperatives with the words in the box. Change the underlined words.

backward	bottom	~~down~~	in	late	~~left~~	light	loudly
low	off	shut	slowly	small	tight	up	white

Affirmative

1. Bend your <u>right</u> leg.

2. *Look down.*

3. Lean <u>forward</u>.

4. _____

5. Breathe <u>out</u>.

6. _____

7. Speak <u>softly</u>.

8. _____

9. Wear <u>loose</u> clothes.

10. _____

11. _____

12. Turn the lights <u>on</u>.

13. _____

14. _____

15. Come <u>early</u>.

16. Lock the <u>top</u> lock.

Negative

1. *Don't bend your left leg.*

2. Don't look <u>up</u>.

3. _____

4. Don't take a <u>big</u> step.

5. _____

6. Don't count <u>quickly</u>.

7. _____

8. Don't keep your eyes <u>open</u>.

9. _____

10. Don't wear a <u>black</u> T-shirt.

11. Don't wear <u>heavy</u> clothes.

12. _____

13. Don't turn the music <u>down</u>.

14. Don't put the heat on <u>high</u>.

15. _____

16. _____

2 | AFFIRMATIVE AND NEGATIVE IMPERATIVES

Ada, a student, is asking her friends for directions to Jim's Gym. Look at the map and complete the conversation. Use the affirmative or negative imperative form of the verbs in the box.

~~ask~~	be	continue	cross	give	go	have	make
pass	ride	show	stop	~~take~~	turn	walk	work

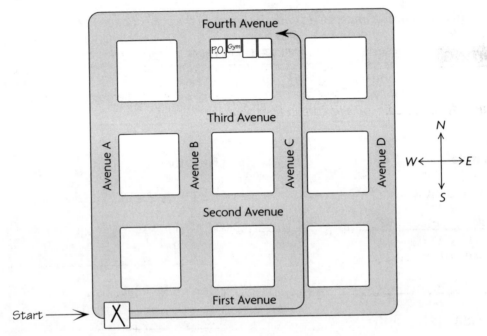

ADA: Hi, guys. How are you doing?

BOB: Hey, Ada. What's up?

ADA: I'm going to take an exercise class at Jim's Gym. Do you know how to get there?

BOB: Jim's Gym? _____*Ask*_____ Chen. He's taking a class there.
   1.

ADA: I didn't know that. Which bus do you take to the gym, Chen?

CHEN: Oh, _____*don't take*_____ the bus! It's not far from here.
   2.

   _____ or _____ your bike. It's good exercise!
   3.   **4.**

ADA: I'll walk. How do I get there? _____ me on this map, OK?
   5.

CHEN: Sure. _____ me the map and I'll show you. _____ two blocks
   6.   **7.**

   east on First Avenue.

ADA: East? You mean turn left?

CHEN: No. _____ left. Go right when you leave the building. OK? Then
    8.
_____ a left turn when you get to Avenue C. _____ on Avenue
    9.   10.
C, but _____ when you reach Fourth Avenue. _____ Fourth
    11.   12.
Avenue. It's another left at Fourth. But _____ careful. Jim's Gym is small,
                                            13.
and it's easy to miss. _____ the post office. The gym is right before it.
                            14.

ADA: Thanks.

CHEN: Sure. _____ fun! _____ too hard!
            15.   16.

3 | EDITING

Read Ada's note to her roommate. There are six mistakes in the use of imperatives. The first mistake is already corrected. Find and correct five more.

Sarah

                                    Call
Your mother called. ~~Calls~~ her at your sister's tonight.

Don't call after 10:00, though.

I went to the gym.

Wash please the dishes and threw out the trash.

If anyone calls for me, takes a message.

Thanks a lot and has a good evening!

A.

4 | PERSONALIZATION

Draw a map and give directions to a place near you. Use your own paper.

Simple Past

1 | SPELLING: REGULAR AND IRREGULAR VERBS

Write the simple past form of the verbs.

Base Form	Simple Past	Base Form	Simple Past
1. answer	answered	16. look	_____
2. begin	began	17. meet	_____
3. buy	bought	18. move	_____
4. catch	caught	19. need	_____
5. come	came	20. open	_____
6. die	died	21. put	_____
7. do	did	22. read	_____
8. feel	felt	23. say	_____
9. find	found	24. see	_____
10. get	got	25. take	_____
11. give	gave	26. think	_____
12. have	had	27. understand	_____
13. hurry	hurried	28. vote	_____
14. kiss	kissed	29. win	_____
15. live	lived	30. write	_____

31. The past of *be* is _____ or _____.

2 | AFFIRMATIVE AND NEGATIVE STATEMENTS: *BE*

Look at the chart of famous writers of the past. Complete the sentences with **was**, **wasn't**, **were**, *and* **weren't**.

ISAAK BABEL	1894–1941	Russia	short-story writer, playwright*
SIMONE DE BEAUVOIR	1908–1966	France	novelist,** essayist***
GIOVANNI BOCCACCIO	1313–1375	Italy	poet, storyteller
KAREL ČAPEK	1890–1938	Czechoslovakia	novelist, essayist
AGATHA CHRISTIE	1890–1976	England	mystery writer
LORRAINE HANSBERRY	1930–1965	United States	playwright
NAZIM HIKMET	1902–1963	Turkey	poet, playwright, novelist
LUCY M. MONTGOMERY	1874–1942	Canada	poet, novelist
PABLO NERUDA	1904–1973	Chile	poet

* A *playwright* writes plays.
** A *novelist* writes novels (books that are fiction).
*** An *essayist* writes essays (short pieces of writing about a topic).

1. Simone de Beauvoir _____*wasn't*_____ a French poet.

   She _____*was*_____ a French novelist.

2. Giovanni Boccaccio _____ born in 1313.

3. Lucy M. Montgomery and Lorraine Hansberry _____ South American writers.

   They _____ North American writers.

4. Karel Čapek _____ a poet.

5. Pablo Neruda _____ from Chile.

6. Agatha Christie _____ American.

   She _____ British.

7. Isaak Babel _____ Russian.

   He _____ French.

8. Nazim Hikmet _____ from Russia.

   He _____ from Turkey.

9. Babel and Hikmet _____ both playwrights.

10. Pablo Neruda and Simone de Beauvoir _____ both born in the early 1900s.

3 | QUESTIONS AND ANSWERS WITH THE PAST OF *BE*

Use **was** *and* **wasn't** *and the words in parentheses to write questions about the writers in Exercise 2. Look at the chart in Exercise 2 and answer the questions.*

1. (Lorraine Hansberry / a playwright)

   A: *Was Lorraine Hansberry a playwright?* _____

   B: *Yes, she was.* _____

2. (Where / Simone de Beauvoir from)

   A: _____

   B: _____

3. (What nationality / Pablo Neruda)

   A: _____

   B: _____

4. (Who / Boccaccio)

   A: _____

   B: _____

5. (Agatha Christie / French)

   A: _____

   B: _____

6. (What nationality / Lucy M. Montgomery)

   A: _____

   B: _____

7. (Nazim Hikmet / a poet)

   A: _____

   B: _____

8. (When / Karel Čapek / born)

   A: _____

   B: _____

9. (Who / Isaak Babel)

   A: _____

   B: _____

4 | AFFIRMATIVE STATEMENTS

Complete the following short biographies with the simple past form of the verbs in the boxes.

| ~~be~~ | begin | die | grow up | love | move | teach | use | write |

A.

Béla Bartók (1881–1945) _____was_____ one of the most famous
1.
composers of the 20th century. Born in Hungary, he ____grow up____
2.
in a musical family. His mother ____Tought____ him how to play
3.
the piano, and at the age of nine he ____began____ to write music.
4.
Bartók ____loved____ the folk music of his native country. He
5.
____used____ these folk tunes, and folk music from other Eastern
6.
European countries, in his own work. In addition to his compositions for musical instruments, he
also ____wroted____ an opera and a ballet. Bartók ____moved____ to the United States
7.   8.
in 1940 and ____died____ there at the age of 64.
9.

| be | begin | die | have | love | marry | paint | plan | study | teach |

B.

Frida Kahlo (1907–1954) _____ one of the most famous
1.
Mexican painters. At first she _____ to be a doctor, but after
2.
a serious accident she _____ painting pictures of her family
3.
and friends from her bed. She also _____ pictures
4.
of herself. Kahlo never _____ art in school. She
5.
_____ herself how to paint, and people _____
6.   7.
her work. In 1929 she ____Marryd____ Diego Rivera, another very famous Mexican painter.
8.
Unfortunately, Kahlo ____have____ a lot of serious medical problems, and she
9.
_____ at the age of 47.
10.

(continued)

| be | build | fly | last | take place | watch |

C.

Orville Wright (1871–1948) and **Wilbur Wright** (1867–1912)

_____*were*_____ American airplane inventors. The two brothers
        1.

_____*builded*_____ their first planes in their bicycle shop in Ohio.
        2.

On December 17, 1903, Orville _____*flew*_____ their plane,
                                          3.

Flyer 1, a distance of 120 feet. Wilbur, four other men, and a boy

_____*watch*_____ from the ground below. This first controlled, power-driven flight
        4.

_____*took*_____ near Kitty Hawk, North Carolina. It _____*lasted*_____ only about
        5.   6.

12 seconds.

5 | QUESTIONS AND ANSWERS

Use the words in parentheses and the simple past to write questions about the people in Exercise 4. Look at the information in Exercise 4 and answer the questions.

Biography A

1. (When / Béla Bartók / live)

   A: _When did Béla Bartók live?_

   B: _He lived from 1881 to 1945._

2. (Where / he / grow up)

   A: _When did grow up_

   B: _he grow up (CNJOR)_

3. (What / he / do)

   A: _What did_

   B: _he playing the pian_

4. (he / spend / his whole life in Hungary)

   A: _did hes spend his_

   B: _____

Biography B

5. (Frida Kahlo / plan to be a painter)

A: _did_

B: _She poзin to be a docteur_

6. (When / she / begin painting)

A: _when did she begane a paxting_

B: _She painted pcteur hell samiti_

7. (What / she / paint)

A: _____

B: _____

8. (When / she / die)

A: _What dale She_

B: _the BV_

Biography C

9. (Where / the Wright brothers / build their first planes)

A: _thei Plaite_

B: _the BUil_

10. (both brothers / fly the *Flyer 1*)

A: _did both brothe flyer 1_

B: _dve'R both brother fly_

11. (Where / the first controlled flight / take place)

A: _the did/le contRoll flight place_

B: _the first contRoll took keni work noth coroli control_

12. (How long / the flight / last)

A: _the flight last about the first control_

B: _____

6 | NEGATIVE STATEMENTS

There were a lot of similarities between the Wright brothers, but there were also differences.
Complete the chart about the differences between Orville and Wilbur.

Orville	**Wilbur**
1. Orville talked a lot.	*Wilbur didn't talk a lot.* ____
2. *Orville didn't spend a lot of time alone.* ____	Wilbur spent a lot of time alone.
3. ____	Wilbur had serious health problems.
4. Orville grew a moustache.	____
5. ____	Wilbur lost most of his hair.
6. Orville took courses in Latin.	____
7. Orville liked to play jokes.	____
8. Orville dressed very fashionably.	____
9. Orville played the guitar.	____
10. ____	Wilbur built the first glider.
11. ____	Wilbur made the first attempts to fly.
12. ____	Wilbur chose the location of Kitty Hawk.
13. Orville had a lot of patience.	____
14. Orville lived a long life.	____

7 | EDITING

Read this student's short biography of a famous person. There are six mistakes in the use of
the simple past. The first mistake is already corrected. Find and correct five more.

                                    was
Pablo Neruda (1904–1973) ~~were~~ a famous poet, political activist,
and diplomat. He was born in Parral, Chile. When he was 17, he gone to
Santiago to continue his education. He did not finished, but he soon
published his first book. Neruda spends the next several decades traveling
and continuing to write poetry. In 1971, while he was Chile's ambassador to France, he
winned the Nobel Prize in literature. He dead two years later.

Past Progressive and Simple Past

1 | AFFIRMATIVE AND NEGATIVE STATEMENTS WITH THE PAST PROGRESSIVE

Frank Cotter is a financial manager. Read his schedule. Use the affirmative or negative past progressive to complete the sentences.

	April 10
	Wednesday
9:00–10:00	meet with Ms. Jacobs
10:00–11:00	write financial reports
11:00–12:00	answer correspondence
12:00–1:00	eat lunch with Mr. Webb at Sol's Cafe
1:00–3:00	attend lecture at City University
3:00–4:00	discuss budget with Alan
4:00–5:00	return phone calls

1. At 9:30, Mr. Cotter _____*was meeting*_____ with Ms. Jacobs.

2. At 9:30, he _____ financial reports.

3. At 11:30, he _____ correspondence.

4. At 12:30, he and Mr. Webb _____ lunch.

(continued)

5. They _____ at Frank's Diner.

6. At 2:00, he _____ a lecture.

7. At 3:30, he and Alan _____ sales reports.

8. They _____ the budget.

9. At 4:30, he _____ correspondence.

10. He _____ phone calls.

2 | QUESTIONS AND ANSWERS WITH THE PAST PROGRESSIVE

Use the words in parentheses to write questions. Look at the schedule in Exercise 1 and write the answers. Use the past progressive.

1. (Mr. Cotter / meet / with Mr. Webb at 9:30)

   A: *Was Mr. Cotter meeting with Mr. Webb at 9:30?* _____

   B: *No, he wasn't.* _____

2. (What / he / do at 9:30)

   A: _____

   B: _____

3. (Mr. Cotter / write police reports at 10:30)

   A: _____

   B: _____

4. (What kind of reports / he / write)

   A: _____

   B: _____

5. (What / he / do at 11:30)

   A: _____

   B: _____

6. (he / have lunch at 12:00)

   A: _____

   B: _____

7. (Who / eat lunch with him)

   A: _____

   B: _____

8. (Where / they / have lunch)

   A: _____

   B: _____

9. (Who / he / talk to at 3:30)

   A: _____

   B: _____

10. (What / they / discuss)

   A: _____

   B: _____

3 | STATEMENTS WITH THE PAST PROGRESSIVE AND SIMPLE PAST

Read this newspaper article. Complete the story with the past progressive or simple past form of the verbs in parentheses.

HIT AND RUN

Last Friday at 5:30 P.M., a blue Honda Accord _____*hit*_____ 35-year-old Lisa
1. (hit)

Coleman while she _____ the street at Broadway and 10th Avenue.
2. (cross)

Witnesses say that the car _____ and _____ at the red light.
3. (speed)   **4. (not stop)**

   Frank Cotter, a financial manager at Smith Webber, _____ on his way
5. (be)

home from work when he _____ the accident. "I _____ along
6. (see)   **7. (walk)**

Broadway when I _____ this blue Honda. I _____ it because
8. (see)   **9. (notice)**

it _____ very fast. When it _____ the intersection, the driver
10. (go)   **11. (reach)**

_____ right through the red light. Seconds later, the car _____
12. (go)   **13. (hit)**

the pedestrian. I immediately _____ my cell phone and _____
14. (take out)   **15. (call)**

the police. The driver _____."
16. (not stop)

(continued)

The accident _____ 17. (happen) just a few blocks from General Hospital, and the ambulance _____ 18. (come) quickly. When it _____ 19. (get) to the scene of the accident, Coleman _____ 20. (lie) on the ground. She _____ 21. (bleed) from a head wound, but she _____ 22. (be) conscious and the police _____ 23. (question) her about the accident.

Coleman _____ 24. (say) that she _____ 25. (cross) the street when the car _____ 26. (go) through the light and _____ 27. (knock) her down. "It all _____ 28. (happen) so quickly," she said. "I _____ 29. (have) a green light, and I _____ 30. (cross) the street when all of a sudden—boom! I _____ 31. (not see) the car."

Coleman _____ 32. (break) her arm and _____ 33. (have) some injuries to her head, but fortunately, they _____ 34. (not be) very serious. Police are still looking for the driver of the Honda.

4 | QUESTIONS WITH THE PAST PROGRESSIVE AND SIMPLE PAST

The police are interviewing another witness to the accident. Use the words in parentheses and the past progressive or simple past to write the interview questions.

1. (What / you / do / when the accident / happen)

   OFFICER: *What were you doing when the accident happened?*

   WITNESS: I was riding my bike home from school when I heard a loud noise.

2. (What / you / do / when you / hear the noise)

   OFFICER: _____

   WITNESS: I got off my bike and looked in the direction of the sound.

3. (What / you / see / when you / look in the direction of the sound)

   OFFICER: _____

   WITNESS: I saw a car—a blue Honda.

4. (Where / you / stand / when you / see the Honda)

   OFFICER: _____

   WITNESS: I was at the corner of Broadway and 10th.

5. (the driver / stop / when the accident / occur)

   OFFICER: _____

   WITNESS: No. The driver didn't stop.

6. (What / happen / next)

   OFFICER: _____

   WITNESS: I tried to get the license plate number, but the car was moving too fast.

7. (you / get a look at the driver / while he / drive away)

   OFFICER: _____

   WITNESS: No, I didn't. I don't even know if it was a man or a woman.

8. (What / the victim / do / when the car / hit her)

   OFFICER: _____

   WITNESS: I don't know. I didn't see her before the car hit her.

UNIT 5 Used to

1 | AFFIRMATIVE STATEMENTS

Life in many countries isn't the way it used to be. Complete the chart.

In the Past	**Now**
1. *People used to ride* horses.	People ride in cars.
2. _____ by candlelight.	People read by electric light.
3. _____ over open fires.	People cook in microwave ovens.
4. _____ all of their clothes by hand.	People wash most of their clothes in washing machines.
5. _____ manual typewriters.	People use word processors and computers.
6. _____ weeks to get a message to another country.	It takes just a few seconds.

2 | AFFIRMATIVE AND NEGATIVE STATEMENTS

Read the sentences about the assistant manager of a California bank, Yoko Shimizu.
*Complete the sentences with the correct form of **used to** and the verbs in parentheses.*

1. Yoko _____*used to be*_____ a full-time student. Now she has a job at a bank.
   (be)

2. She _____ with a computer. Now she uses one every day.
   (work)

3. She _____ a car. Now she owns a 2004 Toyota Corolla.
   (have)

4. Yoko _____ the bus to work. Now she drives.
   (take)

5. The bus _____ crowded. These days it's hard to find a seat.
   (be)

6. Yoko _____ in New York. Then she moved to Los Angeles.
   (live)

7. She _____ Los Angeles. Now she thinks it's a nice city.
   (like)

8. She _____ a lot of people in Los Angeles. Now she has a lot of
   (know)
   friends there.

9. She _____ to New York several times a year. These days she doesn't
   (return)
   go there very often.

10. She _____ a lot of phone calls. Now she sends a lot of e-mails instead.
    (make)

3 | QUESTIONS AND ANSWERS

Use **used to** and the words in parentheses to write questions about Lisa White. Look at the
two ID cards to write the answers.

1. (live in California)

   A: _Did she use to live in California?_ _____

   B: _No, she didn't._ _____

2. Lisa recently moved to Los Angeles. (Where / live)

   A: _____

   B: _____

3. Lisa lives in a house. (live in a house)

   A: _____

   B: _____

4. This is her first job. (What / do)

   A: _____

   B: _____

(continued)

5. (Which school / attend)

A: _____

B: _____

6. Lisa looks very different from before. She has short hair. (have long hair)

A: _____

B: _____

7. (wear glasses)

A: _____

B: _____

8. Lisa's last name is different from before. (be married)

A: _____

B: _____

4 | EDITING

*Read this student's journal entry. There are eight mistakes in the use of **used to**. The first mistake is already corrected. Find and correct seven more.*

Sunday, Oct. 5

Today I ran into an old classmate. We used to be in the same science class. In fact, we used
to ~~studied~~ study together for tests. He was a very good student, and he always uses to get A's. At
first I almost didn't recognize Jason! He looked so different. He used to had very dark hair.
Now he's almost all gray. He also used to being a little heavy. Now he's quite thin. And he was
wearing a suit and tie! I couldn't believe it. He never use to dress that way. He only used to
wore jeans! His personality seemed different too. He didn't used to talk very much. Now he
seems very outgoing. I wonder what he thought of me! I'm sure I look and act different from
the way I was used to too!

5 | PERSONALIZATION

Write five sentences about how your life used to be different from the way it is now. Use
used to *and* **didn't use to**. *Use your own paper.*

Future

1 | AFFIRMATIVE STATEMENTS WITH *BE GOING TO*

Read the situations. Use the words in the box and a form of **be going to** *or*
not be going to *to write predictions or guesses.*

crash	eat lunch	get a ticket	get gas
make a left turn	rain	~~take a trip~~	wash the car

1. Professor Starr is carrying two suitcases toward his car.

   He's going to take a trip.

2. Ms. Marshall has a bucket of water, soap, and a sponge.

   _____

3. Mr. and Mrs. Johnson are driving into an Exxon service station.

   _____

4. Fred is driving behind a woman in a black sports car. Her left indicator light is flashing.

   _____

5. Tiffany is driving 70 miles per hour in a 50-mile-per-hour zone. A police officer is right behind her.

   _____

6. A blue Ford is driving directly toward a white Toyota. They don't have time to stop.

   _____

7. It's noon. The Smiths are driving into a Burger King parking lot.

   _____

8. The sky is full of dark clouds.

   _____

2 | QUESTIONS WITH *BE GOING TO*

Use the words in parentheses to write questions. Use **be going to**.

1. (What / you / do this summer)

   A: *What are you going to do this summer?* _____

   B: My wife and I are going to take a trip to San Francisco.

2. (How long / you / stay)

   A: _____

   B: Just for a week.

3. (you / stay at a hotel)

   A: _____

   B: Yes. We're staying at a hotel in North Beach.

4. (What / you / do in San Francisco)

   A: _____

   B: Oh, the usual, I suppose. Sightseeing and shopping.

5. (you / visit Fisherman's Wharf)

   A: _____

   B: Yes. We're going to take one of those city bus tours.

6. (your daughter / go with you)

   A: _____

   B: No, she's going to attend summer school. Our son isn't going either.

7. (What / he / do)

   A: _____

   B: He got a job at an Italian restaurant.

8. (When / you / leave)

   A: _____

   B: June 11.

   A: Have a good trip.

   B: Thanks.

3 | AFFIRMATIVE AND NEGATIVE STATEMENTS WITH *BE GOING TO*

Look at Professor and Mrs. Starr's boarding passes. Then read the sentences. All of them have incorrect information. Correct the information.

1. Professor Starr is going to go to Los Angeles.

   He isn't going to go to Los Angeles.

   He's going to go to San Francisco.

2. He's going to take the train.

   _____

   _____

3. He's going to travel alone.

   _____

   _____

4. The Starrs are going to leave from Chicago.

   _____

   _____

(continued)

5. They're going to fly US Airways.

   _____

   _____

6. They're going to leave on July 11.

   _____

   _____

7. They're going to take Flight 149.

   _____

   _____

8. The plane is going to depart at 7:00 A.M.

   _____

   _____

9. The Starrs are going to sit apart.

   _____

   _____

10. Mrs. Starr is going to sit in Seat 15B.

    _____

    _____

4 | AFFIRMATIVE AND NEGATIVE STATEMENTS, QUESTIONS, AND SHORT ANSWERS WITH *WILL*

Mrs. Starr is reading an interview about personal robots in the airplane magazine.
Complete the interview with the verbs in parentheses and **will** *or* **won't**.

INTERVIEWER: We all know that robots are already working in factories. But tell us something

about the future. _____*Will*_____ people _____*have*_____ robots at home?
                                                    1. (have)

SCIENTIST: They already do! There are, for example, small robots that vacuum the floor. I

believe that before too long, personal robots _____ as common in
                                                        2. (become)

the home as personal computers are today.

INTERVIEWER: _____ they _____ the computer?
                                          3. (replace)

SCIENTIST: No, they _____ the computer, but one day robots _____

                4. (replace)

    probably _____ computers.

           5. (operate)

INTERVIEWER: That's amazing! What other things _____ personal robots

    _____?

      6. (do)

SCIENTIST: Well, for one thing, they _____ complete home entertainment

                  7. (be)

    centers. They _____, they _____ . . .

            8. (sing)   **9. (dance)**

INTERVIEWER: _____ they _____ jokes?

                   10. (tell)

SCIENTIST: Yes, they _____! But, as with humans, they _____

             11.

    always _____ funny!

      12. (be)

INTERVIEWER: What else _____ personal robots _____?

                       13. (do)

    _____ they _____ more serious uses?

                 14. (have)

SCIENTIST: Yes, they _____. Robots _____ probably

           15.

    _____ care for this country's aging population. I don't believe they

    16. (help)

    _____ people, but they _____ some of the more

    17. (replace)   **18. (perform)**

    routine activities such as making the bed and loading the dishwasher.

INTERVIEWER: It all sounds great. Do you predict any problems?

SCIENTIST: Unfortunately, yes. Some people _____ happy with the spread of

                   19. (be)

    robots. Not everyone's life _____. Some people _____

                20. (improve)   **21. (lose)**

    their jobs to robots. And other people _____ criminal robots!

                    22. (create)

INTERVIEWER: _____ we _____ new laws to deal with robotic crime?

                 23. (need)

SCIENTIST: I'm afraid so.

INTERVIEWER: Tell me, how _____ these personal robots _____?

                        24. (look)

SCIENTIST: Well, they _____ exactly like humans, but they _____

           25. (look)   **26. (resemble)**

    us quite a bit.

INTERVIEWER: And when _____ all this _____?

                 27. (happen)

SCIENTIST: Soon! I predict it _____ in the very near future.

      28. (happen)

5 | RECOGNIZING THE SIMPLE PRESENT AND PRESENT PROGRESSIVE WHEN THEY REFER TO THE FUTURE

Read this article about a new play. Underline the simple present and present progressive verbs only when they refer to the future.

CURTAIN CALL

A NEW PLAY

Next Wednesday <u>is</u> the first performance of *Robots*. Melissa Robins is playing the leading role. Robins, who lives in Italy and who is vacationing in Greece, is not available for an interview at this time. She is, however, appearing on Channel 8's "Theater Talk" sometime next month.

Although shows traditionally begin at 8:00 P.M., *Robots*, because of its length, starts half an hour earlier.

Immediately following the opening-night performance, the company is having a reception in the theater lounge. Tickets are still available. Call 555-6310 for more information.

6 | CONTRAST OF FUTURE FORMS

Some people are flying to San Francisco. Read the conversations and circle the most appropriate future forms.

1. **A:** Do you know our arrival time?

   B: According to the schedule, (we arrive) / we'll arrive at 10:45.

2. **A:** Why did you bring your computer with you?

   B: <u>I'll do / I'm going to do</u> some work while we're away.

3. **A:** I'm thirsty. I think <u>I'll ask / I'm asking</u> for a soda.

   B: Good idea. There's the flight attendant.

4. **A:** Excuse me. Do you know what the weather is like in San Francisco?

   B: It's clear now, but <u>it's raining / it's going to rain</u> tomorrow.

5. **A:** Oh, good! <u>They'll show / They're showing</u> the new *Star Wars* on today's flight.

   B: Great! I missed it when it was playing in the theaters.

6. **A:** Just look at those dark clouds!

   B: I see. It looks like <u>we're going to have / we'll have</u> some rough weather ahead.

7. **A:** Hold on to your cup! It looks like <u>it will spill / it's going to spill</u>.

   B: I've got it. This sure is a bumpy flight!

   A: I know. <u>I'll be / I'm</u> glad to be back on the ground again.

8. **A:** I'm tired. I think <u>I'll take / I'm taking</u> a little nap. Wake me when the movie begins.

   B: OK. Sweet dreams.

9. **A:** It's 11:00 P.M. already!

   B: I know. <u>We're going to arrive / We arrive</u> late.

   A: That's too bad.

10. **A:** You know, I don't think the airport buses run after midnight.

    B: I'm afraid you're right. How <u>are we going to get / are we getting</u> to the hotel?

11. **A:** Hmmm. No buses. Well, that's no problem. <u>We'll take / We're going to take</u> a taxi.

    B: Do you think there <u>will still be / are still</u> taxis in front of the terminal so late?

    A: Oh, sure.

    B: That's good.

12. **A:** I missed the announcement. What did the captain say?

    B: He said, "Fasten your seat belts. <u>We're landing / We'll land</u> in about 10 minutes."

    A: Great.

13. **C:** How long <u>are you going to stay / will you stay</u> in San Francisco?

    A: Just a week.

    C: Well, enjoy yourselves. And thank you for flying FairAir.

14. **A:** Maybe <u>we'll see / we're seeing</u> you on the return flight!

    C: Maybe!

7 | EDITING

Read this boy's postcard. There are five mistakes in the use of future forms. The first mistake is already corrected. Find and correct four more. Note: There may be more than one way to correct the mistakes!

Hi!

~~I going~~ *I'm going* to stay here for a week with my parents.

We have a lot of fun things planned. Tomorrow night we'll see a play called *Robots*. Mom already bought the tickets for it. The play begins at 7:30, and before that we have dinner on Fisherman's Wharf. Right now we're sitting in Golden Gate Park, but we have to leave. The sky is getting very dark. It will rain!

I call you soon.

Jason

8 | PERSONALIZATION

Write a note to a friend. Tell your friend about your future plans.

_____

_____

_____

_____

_____

_____

_____

_____

Future Time Clauses

1 | SIMPLE PRESENT OR FUTURE WITH *WILL*

Complete the clauses with the correct form of the verbs in parentheses. Use the future or the simple present. Then match the time clauses to the main clauses.

Time Clause

h 1. When the alarm clock _____*rings*_____
(ring)
at 7:00 A.M.,

____ 2. After she _____,
(get up)

____ 3. As soon as the coffee _____ ready,
(be)

____ 4. While they _____ breakfast,
(eat)

____ 5. When they _____ breakfast,
(finish)

____ 6. After her husband _____ the
(wash)
dinner dishes,

____ 7. As soon as they _____ the car,
(get in)

____ 8. Until he _____ his driver's
(get)
license,

____ 9. Until the rain _____,
(stop)

____ 10. By the time the day _____ over,
(be)

Main Clause

a. they _____ very
(be)
tired.

b. she _____.
(drive)

c. they _____ it.
(drink)

d. they _____ their
(fasten)
seat belts.

e. she _____ them.
(dry)

f. they _____ their
(need)
umbrellas.

g. they _____ dishes.
(do)

h. she _____*'ll get up*_____.
(get up)

i. she _____ a shower.
(take)

j. they _____ the
(read)
morning newspaper.

2 | SIMPLE PRESENT OR FUTURE (*WILL / BE GOING TO*) AND TIME EXPRESSIONS

Vera is a student. Look at her future plans. Complete the sentences below with the correct form of the verbs in parentheses. Use Vera's plans to choose the correct time expression.

Future Plans

Take the TOEFL* exam
Apply to college for next year
Finish school
Visit Aunt Isabel
Get a summer job and take a computer-
   programming course
Fly to Brazil – Aug. 28
Get married – Sept. 30
Return to the United States
Move into new apartment
Look for a part-time job

*TOEFL® = Test of English as a Foreign Language

1. Vera ___will take___ the TOEFL® exam ___before___ she ___applies___
         (take)   (when / before)   (apply)
   to college.

2. Vera _____ to college _____ she _____ school.
         (apply)   (before / after)   (finish)

3. _____ she _____ school, she _____ her aunt.
     (Before / After)   (finish)   (visit)

4. _____ she _____ at a summer job, she _____ a
     (Before / While)   (work)   (take)
   course in computer programming.

5. She _____ her aunt Isabel _____ she _____ a job.
       (visit)   (while / before)   (get)

6. _____ she _____ the course, she _____ to Brazil.
     (Before / When)   (finish)   (fly)

7. She _____ _____ she _____ in Brazil.
       (get married)   (when / before)   (be)

8. She _____ to the United States _____ she _____.
       (return)   (before / after)   (get married)

9. She _____ into a new apartment _____ she _____
       (move)   (when / while)   (return)
   to the United States.

10. _____ she _____ into a new apartment, she _____
     (Before / After)   (move)   (look for)
    a part-time job.

3 | SENTENCE COMBINING

Combine these pairs of sentences. Use the future or the simple present form of the verb.
Remember to use commas when necessary.

1. Vera will finish her summer job. Then she's going to fly to Brazil.

   _____*Vera is going to fly to Brazil*_____ after _____*she finishes her summer job.*_____

2. Vera will save enough money from her job. Then she's going to buy a plane ticket.

   As soon as _____

3. Vera's going to buy presents for her family. Then she's going to go home.

   Before _____

4. Vera will arrive at the airport. Her father will be there to drive her home.

   When _____

5. Vera and her father will get home. They'll immediately have dinner.

   As soon as _____

6. They'll finish dinner. Then Vera will give her family the presents.

   _____ after _____

7. Vera's brother will wash the dishes, and Vera's sister will dry them.

   _____ while _____

8. The whole family will stay up talking. Then the clock will strike midnight.

   _____ until _____

9. They'll all feel very tired. Then they'll go to bed.

   By the time _____

10. Vera's head will hit the pillow, and she'll fall asleep immediately.

    _____ as soon as _____

11. Vera will wake up the next morning. She'll call her friends.

    When _____

12. She'll have breakfast. Then she'll see her friends.

    _____ as soon as _____

4 | EDITING

Read Vera's e-mail. There are eight mistakes in the use of future time clauses. The first one is already corrected. Find and correct seven more. Remember to look at punctuation!

Hi, Monica!

I'm really looking forward to your arrival tomorrow. Before you ~~will~~ know it, you'll be here!

After I will pick you up at the airport, we'll go straight to my parents' house. My mother is

going to make a special dinner, but before we have dinner, you and I go for a drive with

Paulo. Rio is a beautiful city, and we can't wait to show you some of the sights. After we will

have dinner some of our friends will come over to meet you.

Let's talk on the phone once more, before you're going to leave. I'm going out for a few

hours, but I call you as soon as I get back.

I'll speak to you soon.

Vera

5 | PERSONALIZATION

Complete these sentences with information about your own future plans.

1. As soon as _____, I'll go to bed.

2. Before I take a break, _____.

3. Until _____, I'll stay in school.

4. When I save enough money, _____.

5. I won't _____ before I _____.

6. _____ after _____.

7. _____ while _____.

8. When I finish this exercise, _____.

Wh- Questions: Subject and Object

1 | QUESTIONS ABOUT THE SUBJECT

Ask questions about the words in italics. Use **What**, **Whose**, **Who**, *or* **How many**.

1. *Something* happened last night.

   What happened last night?

2. *Someone's* phone rang at midnight.

   _____

3. *Someone* was calling for Michelle.

   _____

4. *Someone* was having a party.

   _____

5. *Some number of* people left the party.

   _____

6. *Something* surprised them.

   _____

7. *Someone's* friend called the police.

   _____

8. *Some number of* police arrived.

   _____

9. *Something* happened next.

   _____

10. *Someone* told the police about a theft.

   _____

(continued)

11. *Someone's* jewelry disappeared.

_____

12. *Some number of* necklaces vanished.

_____

2 | QUESTIONS ABOUT THE OBJECT AND *WHY, WHEN,* OR *WHERE*

Use the cues to write questions about Megan Knight, an accountant in Texas. Then match the questions and answers.

Questions	Answers
_e_ **1.** Where / she / live?	**a.** Two years.
Where does she live?	**b.** By bus.
_____ **2.** How many rooms / her apartment / have?	**c.** The first of the month.
_____	**d.** Ling, Jackson, & Drew, Inc.
_____ **3.** How much rent / she / pay?	**e.** In Texas.
_____	**f.** Five and a half.
_____ **4.** When / she / pay the rent?	**g.** She's an accountant.
_____	**h.** Her sister.
_____ **5.** Who / she / live with?	**i.** Because she doesn't like to drive.
_____	**j.** About $800 a month.
_____ **6.** What / she / do?	
_____	
_____ **7.** Which company / she / work for?	
_____	
_____ **8.** How long / she / plan to stay there?	
_____	
_____ **9.** How / she / get to work?	
_____	
_____ **10.** Why / she / take the bus?	
_____	

3 | QUESTIONS ABOUT THE SUBJECT AND OBJECT AND *WHY, WHEN,* OR *WHERE*

Megan wrote a letter to her friend Janice. The letter got wet, and now Janice can't read some parts of it. What questions does Janice ask to get the missing information?

Dear Janice,

Hi! I just moved to ▨▨▨▨▨▨. I left Chicago because ▨▨▨▨▨.
1.   **2.**
▨▨▨ moved with me, and we are sharing an apartment. I got a job in a ▨▨▨▨▨.
3.   **4.**
It started ▨▨▨. The people seem nice. Our apartment is great. It has ▨▨▨ rooms.
5.   **6.**
▨▨▨ of the rooms came with carpeting, but two of them have beautiful wood floors. The rent
7.
isn't too high, either. We each pay $ ▨▨ a month.
                      8.

We need to buy some ▨▨▨▨. ▨▨▨'s brother wants to visit her, so we really
9.   **10.**

need an extra bed.

By the way, ▨▨▨ called last Sunday. I also spoke to ▨▨▨. They
11.   **12.**
want to visit us in ▨▨▨. Would you like to come too? Is that a good time for you?
13.
There's plenty of room because ▨▨▨▨▨. Write and let me know.
                              14.

Love,
Megan

1. *Where did you move?*
2. _____
3. _____
4. _____
5. _____
6. _____
7. _____
8. _____
9. _____
10. _____

(continued)

11. _____

12. _____

13. _____

14. _____

4 | PERSONALIZATION

Imagine you are writing to a friend who has just moved. Ask your friend questions about his or her new home.

1. When _____

2. Where _____

3. Why _____

4. How many _____

5. What _____

6. How far _____

7. Which _____

8. Who _____

Reflexive and Reciprocal Pronouns

1 | REFLEXIVE PRONOUNS

Write the reflexive pronouns.

1. I   *myself* _____

2. my grandfather _____

3. the children _____

4. the class _____

5. my aunt _____

6. you _____ OR _____

7. people _____

8. life _____

9. my parents _____

10. we _____

2 | REFLEXIVE AND RECIPROCAL PRONOUNS

Choose the correct pronouns to complete the sentences.

1. Cindi and Jim phone (each other)/ themselves every weekend.

2. They have worked with <u>each other / themselves</u> for five years.

3. Cindi <u>herself / himself</u> has been with the same company for 10 years.

4. It's a nice place. All of the employees consider <u>one another / themselves</u> lucky to be there.

5. They respect <u>each other / each other's</u> opinions.

6. The boss <u>herself / itself</u> is very nice.

7. She tells her employees, "Don't push <u>themselves / yourselves</u> too hard!"

(continued)

8. Cindi enjoys the job <u>herself / itself</u>, but she especially likes her co-workers.

9. My brother and I are considering applying for a job there <u>myself / ourselves</u>.

10. We talk to <u>each other / ourselves</u> about it when we jog together.

3 | REFLEXIVE AND RECIPROCAL PRONOUNS

Gina had a party. Read each conversation and complete the summary. Use the correct form of the verbs in parentheses with an appropriate reflexive or reciprocal pronoun.

1. JOYCE: This party is a lot of fun.

    HANK: I've never danced with so any people in my life!

    SUMMARY: Joyce and Hank _____ *are enjoying themselves* _____.
    (enjoy)

2. RON: We were late because you forgot the address.

    MIA: It's not my fault. You never gave me the slip of paper!

    SUMMARY: Ron and Mia _____.
    (criticize)

3. GINA: I'm so glad you could come. There are food and drinks on that table over there.

    Why don't you take a plate and get some?

    CHEN: Thanks. I will. It all looks delicious.

    SUMMARY: Chen _____.
    (help)

4. AMY: OK, Amy. Now don't be shy. Go over and talk to that guy over there.

    TIM: Come on, Tim. You can do it. She's looking in your direction. Just go on over.

    SUMMARY: Amy and Tim _____.
    (talk)

5. AMY: Hi. I'm Amy.

    TIM: Hi. I'm Tim.

    SUMMARY: Amy and Tim _____.
    (introduce)

6. AMY: So, how do you know Gina?

    TIM: Oh, Gina and I were in the same class. What about you?

    SUMMARY: Amy and Tim _____.
    (talk)

7. PAT: Did you come with Doug?

    LAURA: No. Doug couldn't make it, but he let me use his car.

    SUMMARY: Laura _____.
    (drive)

8. **LIZ:** I'm sorry to hear about your job, Hank.

HANK: I think I didn't take it seriously enough, but I've learned my lesson. I'll do better next time.

SUMMARY: Hank _____.
(blame)

9. **CARA:** You know, I'm really glad we met.

LIZ: Me too. I feel like we've known each other a long time.

SUMMARY: Cara and Liz _____ company.
(enjoy)

10. **LIZ:** It was a wonderful party. Thanks for inviting me.

GINA: Thanks for coming. And thank you for the lovely flowers.

SUMMARY: Liz and Gina _____.
(thank)

4 | EDITING

Read Liz's journal entry. There are eleven mistakes in the use of reflexive and reciprocal pronouns. The first mistake is already corrected. Find and correct ten more.

> April 25
>
>   myself
> I really enjoyed ~~me~~ at Gina's party! Hank was there, and we talked to ourselves
> quite a bit. He's a little depressed about losing his job. The job himself wasn't that great,
> but he needs the money. He's disappointed in himself. He thinks it's all his own fault, and
> he blames him for the whole thing. Hank introduced myself to several of his friends. I
> spoke a lot to this one woman, Cara. We have a lot of things in common, and after just
> an hour, we felt like we had known each other's forever. Cara, himself, is a computer
> programmer, just like me.
>
>   At first I was nervous about going to the party alone. I sometimes feel a little
> uncomfortable when I'm in a social situation by oneself. But this time was different.
> Before I went, I kept telling myself to relax. My roommate, too, kept telling myself, "Don't
> be so hard on you! Just have fun!" That's what I advised Hank to do too. Before we left
> the party, Hank and I promised us to keep in touch. I hope to see him again soon.

10 Phrasal Verbs

1 | PARTICLES

Complete the phrasal verbs with particles from the box. You will use some particles more than once.

back	down	in	off	on	out	over	together	up

Phrasal Verb	**Definition**
1. take _____off_____	*remove*
2. figure _____	*solve*
3. go _____	*continue*
4. call _____	*cancel*
5. call _____	*return a phone call*
6. fill _____	*complete*
7. turn _____	*reject*
8. point _____	*indicate*
9. grow _____	*become an adult*
10. give _____	*quit*
11. help _____	*assist*
12. blow _____	*explode*
13. look _____	*be careful*
14. come _____	*enter*
15. work _____	*exercise*
16. get _____	*return*
17. put _____	*assemble*
18. think _____	*consider*

2 | PHRASAL VERBS

Complete the handout for Professor Cho's class. Use the correct phrasal verbs from the box.

do over	hand in	help out	look over	look up
pick out	pi̶c̶k̶ up	set up	talk over	write up

Science 101   Instructions for Writing the Term Paper   Prof. Cho

- -

1. _____*Pick up*_____ a list of topics from the science department secretary.

2. _____ a topic that interests you. (If you are having problems choosing a topic,

I'll be glad to _____ you _____ .)

3. Go online. Use the Internet to _____ information on your chosen topic.

4. _____ an appointment with me to _____ your topic.

5. _____ your first draft.

6. _____ it _____ carefully. Check for accuracy of facts, spelling,

and grammar errors.

7. _____ your report _____ if necessary.

8. _____ it _____ by May 28.

---

3 | PHRASAL VERBS AND OBJECT PRONOUNS

Complete the conversations between roommates. Use phrasal verbs and pronouns.

1. **A:** I haven't picked up the list of topics for our science paper yet.

   B: I'll _____*pick it up*_____ for you. I'm going to the science

   office this afternoon.

2. **A:** Hey, guys. We've really got to clean up the kitchen. It's a mess.

   B: It's my turn to _____. I'll do it after dinner.

3. **A:** Did you remember to call your mom back?

   B: Oops! I'll _____ tonight.

(continued)

4. **A:** Hey, can you turn down that music? I'm trying to concentrate.

   B: Sorry. I'll _____ right away.

5. **A:** It's after 9:00. Do you think we should wake John up?

   B: Don't _____. He said he wanted to sleep late.

6. **A:** Professor Cho turned down my science topic.

   B: Really? Why did she _____?

7. **A:** When do we have to hand in our reports?

   B: We have to _____ by Friday.

8. **A:** I wanted to drop off my report this afternoon, but I'm not going to have time.

   B: I can _____ for you. I have an appointment

   with Professor Cho at noon.

4 | WORD ORDER

Professor Cho made a list of things to do with her class. Unscramble the words to make sentences. In some cases, more than one answer is possible.

1. the homework problems / back / give

   Give back the homework problems. OR _Give the homework problems back._

2. out / common mistakes / point

   _____

3. them / over / talk

   _____

4. a new problem / out / pick

   _____

5. it / out / work / with the class

   _____

6. up / the results / write

   _____

7. go / to the next unit / on

   _____

8. up / the final exam questions / make

_____

9. them / out / hand

_____

10. study groups / up / set

_____

11. out / them / help

_____

12. Friday's class / off / call

_____

5 | EDITING

Read this student's e-mail. There are eleven mistakes in the use of phrasal verbs. The first mistake is already corrected. Find and correct ten more. A particle in the wrong place counts as one mistake.

Hi, Katy!

How are things going? I'm already into the second month of the spring semester, and I've got a lot of work to do. For science class, I have to write a term paper. The professor made ~~over~~ _up_ a list of possible topics. After looking over them, I think I've picked one out. I'm going to write about chimpanzees. I've already looked some information about them online up. I found up some very interesting facts.

Did you know that their hands look very much like their feet, and that they have fingernails and toenails? Their thumbs and big toes are "opposable." This makes it easy for them to pick things out with both their fingers and toes. Their arms are longer than their legs. This helps

(continued)

out them, too, because they can reach out to fruit growing on thin branches that would not otherwise support their weight. Adult males weigh between 90 and 115 pounds, and they are about four feet high when they stand out.

Like humans, chimpanzees are very social. They travel in groups called "communities." Mothers bring out their chimps, who stay with them until about the age of seven. Even after the chimps grow up, there is still a lot of contact with other chimpanzees.

I could go on, but I need to stop writing now so I can clean out my room (it's a mess!) a little before going to bed. It's late already, and I have to get early up tomorrow morning for my 9:00 class.

Please let me know how you are. Or call me. I'm often out, but if you leave a message, I'll call back you as soon as I can. It would be great to speak to you.

Best,

Tony

Ability:
Can, Could, Be able to

1 | AFFIRMATIVE AND NEGATIVE STATEMENTS WITH *CAN* AND *COULD*

Read about this student's ability in English. Then complete the statements for each item.
(For items 8–10, write complete statements.) Use **can**, **can't**, **could**, *or* **couldn't**.

Student's Name *Fernando Ochoa*

English Language Ability Questionnaire

Skill	Now	Before This Course
1. understand conversational English	✔	✗
2. understand recorded announcements	✗	✗
3. read an English newspaper	✔	✔
4. read an English novel	✗	✗
5. speak on the phone	✔	✗
6. speak with a group of people	✔	✗
7. write an e-mail	✔	✔
8. write a business letter	✗	✗
9. order a meal in English	✔	✔
10. go shopping	✔	✔

---

1. Before this course, he <u>*couldn't understand conversational English.*</u>

Now he <u>*can understand conversational English.*</u>

2. He <u>*couldn't understand recorded anouncements*</u> before the course, and

he still <u>*can't understand recorded anouncements.*</u>

3. He _____ now, and he

_____ before too.

4. He _____ before the course, and

he still _____.

(continued)

51

5. Now he _____, but before the course

   he _____.

6. Before the course, he _____, but

   now he _____.

7. Before the course, he _____.

   He still _____, of course.

8. _____

   _____

9. _____

   _____

10. _____

    _____

   SUMMARY: Fernando _____ do a lot more now than he

   _____ before the course.

2 | QUESTIONS AND ANSWERS WITH *CAN* AND *COULD*

A reporter from the school newspaper is interviewing a new student. Use **can** *or* **could** *and the words in parentheses to write the interview questions and the student's answers.*

1. (speak / any other languages)

   REPORTER: *Can you speak any other languages?* _____

   STUDENT: _____ *Yes, I can.* _____ I speak two other languages.

2. (What languages / speak)

   REPORTER: _____

   STUDENT: Spanish and French.

3. (speak Spanish / when you were a child)

   REPORTER: _____

   STUDENT: _____ I learned it as an adult.

4. (speak French)

REPORTER: _____

STUDENT: _____ We spoke French some of the time at home.

5. (before you came here / understand spoken English)

REPORTER: _____

STUDENT: _____ I didn't understand anything!

6. (understand song lyrics)

REPORTER: What about now? _____

STUDENT: _____ Especially if I listen to them more than once.

7. (before this course / write a business letter in English)

REPORTER: _____

STUDENT: _____ But I used to write in English to my friends.

8. (drive a car before you came here)

REPORTER: So, tell me some more about yourself. _____

_____

STUDENT: _____ I was too young.

9. (drive a car now)

REPORTER: _____

STUDENT: _____ I still haven't learned.

10. (swim)

REPORTER: We're not far from the beach here. _____

STUDENT: _____ I've been swimming since I was a little kid.

11. (surf before you came here)

REPORTER: What about surfing? _____

STUDENT: _____ But I learned to surf the first month I was here.

12. (What / do now / that / you / not do before)

REPORTER: _____

STUDENT: Oh! I _____ a lot of things now that I _____

before.

3 | AFFIRMATIVE AND NEGATIVE STATEMENTS WITH *BE ABLE TO*

Read this article about hearing loss. Complete the article with the correct form of **be able to** *and the verbs in parentheses.*

Living in a Hearing World

There are millions of people who have some degree of hearing loss. There are two major types of hearing loss.

1. **Sound Sensitivity Loss.** People with this kind of loss ___*are not able to hear*___
   1. (not hear)

   soft sounds—a whisper or a bird singing, for example. However, when sounds are loud

   enough, they _____ them correctly.
   2. (interpret)

2. **Sound Discrimination Loss.** People with this particular kind of hearing loss

   _____ one sound from another. As a result of this,
   3. (not distinguish)

   they _____ speech—even when it is loud enough for
   4. (not understand)

   them to hear.

   How do people with hearing disabilities get along in a hearing world? Most people with

   hearing impairments _____ some sounds. With the use of
   5. (hear)

   hearing aids and cochlear implants (devices put in the ear during an operation), many people

   _____ some of their ability to hear. Some people with
   6. (get back)

   hearing disabilities _____ lips. But, at best, lipreading is
   7. (read)

   only 30 to 50 percent effective. Even a good lip-reader _____
   8. (not recognize)

   all the sounds. Just ask someone to silently mouth the words *pat*, *bat*, and *mat*. The

   three words sound different, but they all *look* the same. In addition, the human eye

   _____ fast enough to process speech by vision alone. By
   9. (not work)

   far the most successful form of communication is signing—the use of sign language. People

   with hearing impairments _____ successfully with others
   10. (communicate)

   who know this language.

4 | QUESTIONS AND SHORT ANSWERS WITH *BE ABLE TO*

*Modern technology can make life easier for people with hearing loss. Read this FAQ (frequently asked questions) about assisted-hearing devices. Use **will be able to** to complete the questions and write short answers.*

Q: My daughter has a hearing disability. She's going to have her first child next month.

_____Will____ she _____be able to know_____ when the baby is crying?
                        1. (know)

A: _____Yes, she will._____ She can get a device that flashes lights (so she'll be
                2.
able to see the signal) or vibrates (so she'll be able to feel the signal).

* * * * * *

Q: My nephew can't hear the alarm clock in the morning. I want to buy him a flashing lamp.

_____ he _____ it when he's sleeping?
                        3. (How / see)

A: You can see a strong light through your eyelids—as long as you don't have your head under

the covers!

* * * * * *

Q: I'm thinking of getting a cochlear implant. _____ I _____
                                                                    4. (hear)
"normally" with it?

A: _____ Hearing with an implant is not the same as
                5.
"normal" hearing, but it *can* help a lot.

* * * * * *

Q: I just moved into a new apartment, and I'm having trouble hearing the doorbell.

_____ I _____ this problem without disturbing my
                        6. (How / solve)
neighbors?

A: You can get a system that produces sound in different locations in your apartment—not just

at the front door.

* * * * * *

(continued)

Q: My husband and I both wear hearing aids, and we both love to travel. _____ we

_____ the theater when we're in London next summer?
                    7.(enjoy)

A: _____ Theaters in London use a "loop" system. This
                    8.

system sends sounds directly to your hearing aid (without wires!). You just need to set your

hearing aid to "T." Have a good trip!

---

5 | CONTRAST: *CAN* AND *BE ABLE TO*

Read this article about a well-known actress who is deaf. Complete the story with the correct form of **can, could,** *or* **be able to** *and the verbs in parentheses. Use* **can** *or* **could** *when possible.*

Actress Marlee Matlin _____*could hear*_____ at birth but lost
                                    1.(hear)

her hearing at the age of 18 months as a result of a childhood illness.

By the age of five, she _____ lips. Shortly
                                    2.(read)

after that, she mastered sign language. At first, Matlin felt angry and

frightened by her hearing impairment. "I wanted to be perfect, and I

_____ my deafness," she said during an
            3.(not accept)

interview. With time, however, she learned to accept it.

Matlin began her acting career at the age of eight, when she performed in theater for the deaf.

In 1986, she received an Oscar nomination for best actress in the Hollywood film *Children of a*

Lesser God. In the movie she played the role of an angry woman who was deaf and did not want

to speak. For Matlin, however, speaking is very important. At the Oscar ceremonies, she

_____ her award verbally. It was the first time the public heard her speak.
        4.(accept)

"It's what I wanted to do, because a lot of people all over the world _____
                                                                            5.(see)

me for who I am," she said. Matlin was worried, however. She asked, "What other roles

_____ I _____ in the future?"
                                    6.(do)

Matlin didn't need to worry. She continued to receive important roles in movies and on TV.

One reviewer said "She _____ more saying nothing than most people
                            7.(do)

_____ talking." Today, thanks to intensive speech training, she
        8. (do)

_____ very clearly. In 1994 she _____ something
        9. (speak)   10. (achieve)

for the first time: She played the role of a character who was not deaf. Matlin, in fact, doesn't

think of herself as a "deaf actress." She's an "actress who happens to be deaf." She hopes that in

the future she _____ more roles that are not specifically for people with
                        11. (get)

hearing impairments.

   In addition to her acting career, Matlin is actively trying to improve lives. In 1995, she helped

get an important law passed in the United States. As a result of this law, today most TV sets have

closed-captioning on their screens so that hearing-impaired viewers _____

everything. Matlin does not believe in limits. "I _____ attitudes on
                                                                12. (read)

                                                        13. (change)

deafness and prove we _____ everything—except hear," she said.
                                14. (do)

6 | EDITING

Read this student's composition. There are ten mistakes in the use of **can**, **could**, _and_
be able to. _The first one is already corrected. Find and correct nine more._

> *couldn't*
> Before I came to this country, I ~~can't~~ do many things in English. For example,
> I couldn't follow a conversation if many people were talking at the same time. I
> remember a party I went to. Everyone was speaking English, and I wasn't able
> understand a word! I felt so uncomfortable. Finally, my aunt came to pick me up,
> and I could leave the party.
>
>   Today I can to understand much better. I am taking classes at the adult center.
> My teacher is very good. She can explains things well, and she always gives us
> the chance to talk a lot in class. When I finish this class, I can speak and
> understand a lot better.
>
>   Be able to speak English well is very important to me. I practice a lot at home
> too. When I first came to this country, I can't understand very much TV, but now I
> can to understand much better. In fact, I can do a lot now, and I think in a few more
> months I can do even more.

7 | PERSONALIZATION

Look at the English Language Ability Questionnaire in Exercise 1. Write sentences about your English ability now and before this course.

1. _____
   _____

2. _____
   _____

3. _____
   _____

4. _____
   _____

Permission: *Can, Could, May, Do you mind if*

1 | QUESTIONS AND RESPONSES

Match these classroom questions and responses.

Questions

_d_ **1.** Do you mind if I bring my friends
to class?

_____ **2.** May I ask a question?

_____ **3.** Do you mind if I record the lesson?

_____ **4.** Could I open the window?

_____ **5.** Can we review Unit 4?

_____ **6.** May I leave the room?

_____ **7.** Could we use our dictionaries?

_____ **8.** Could I borrow a pen?

Responses

a. Certainly. The key to the restroom is hanging
on the wall.

b. Not at all. I think it's a good idea.

c. Sure. I hope I can answer it.

d. Sorry, but yes, I do. It's already pretty
crowded.

e. Sure. But remember: You don't have to look
up every word.

f. I'm afraid we can't. We're running out of time.

g. Sure. But please remember to return it.

h. Go right ahead. It's quite warm in here.

2 | QUESTIONS

Read the classroom situations. Complete the questions asking for permission.

1. You want to open the window.

May _I open the window?_____

2. Your whole class wants to review Unit 6.

Could _____

3. You want to borrow a classmate's pen.

Can _____

(continued)

4. You want to look at someone's class notes.

   Do you mind if _____

5. You want to come late to the next class.

   Do you mind if _____

6. Your roommate wants to come to the next class with you.

   Could _____

7. You want to ask a question.

   May _____

8. You and a classmate would like to use a dictionary.

   Can _____

9. You and your classmates want to leave five minutes early.

   Could _____

10. Your sister wants to go on the class trip with the rest of the class.

    Do you mind if _____

3 | PERSONALIZATION

Imagine that you are in class and are in the following situations. Ask your teacher for permission to do something.

1. You don't understand something the teacher is saying.

   _____

2. You don't feel well.

   _____

3. Your cousin (from your country) is going to visit you for a week.

   _____

4. You're having trouble with a paper you're writing.

   _____

Now write your own request.

5. _____

4 | AFFIRMATIVE AND NEGATIVE STATEMENTS

Look at the flyer. Complete the statements with the words in parentheses.

Class Trip

You are invited to our annual class picnic on

Sunday, May 26, at Glenwood State Park.

Food and beverages welcome, but no glass containers, please!

Bus tickets $5.00 (check or cash)

Advance purchase only • No refunds

Bring a friend!

Don't forget your bathing suit! The lake is beautiful.

1. You _____*may bring*_____ a friend.
   (may / bring)

2. You _____ your own food.
   (can / bring)

3. You _____ your own drinks.
   (can / bring)

4. You _____ juice from a glass bottle at the picnic.
   (can / drink)

5. You _____ for your bus ticket by check.
   (can / pay)

6. You _____ for your bus ticket by cash.
   (can / pay)

7. You _____ for your ticket by credit card.
   (may / pay)

8. You _____ your bus ticket on the day of the trip.
   (may / purchase)

9. You _____ a refund.
   (can / get)

10. You _____ in the lake.
    (may / swim)

5 | EDITING

*Read this professor's response to an e-mail from one of his students. (The professor's answers are in **bold** print.) There are six mistakes in making and responding to requests. The first one is already corrected. Find and correct five more.*

Subj: Missed classes—Reply
Date: 04-23-06 11:22:43 EST
From: profwilson@bryant.edu
To: Timbotwo@hotline.com

>>>Timbotwo@hotline.com> 04/23/06 9:05am>>>

Professor Wilson—

I've been sick for the past two days. That's why I missed the last test.
                                                                    take
May I ~~taking~~ a make-up exam?

Yes. If you bring a doctor's note.

If I can take the exam, may I use my calculator during the test?

No, you mayn't! I did not allow calculators during this test.

Could my roommate comes to class and take notes for me on Thursday?

Yes, he could.

Do you mind when he records the class for me?

Not at all. It's fine for him to record the class.

One last thing—I know I missed some handouts. May I have please copies of them?

Sure. I'll give them to your roommate on Thursday.

Thanks a lot.

Tim

Requests: *Can, Could, Will, Would, Would you mind*

| **REQUESTS AND RESPONSES**

Match these office requests and responses.

Requests

Responses

_d_ 1. Could you meet me tomorrow at 8:00 A.M.?

a. I'd be glad to. When do you need it?

____ 2. Will you please type this memo for me?

b. Sure. It is pretty cold in here.

____ 3. Could you show me how to use the scanner?

c. Of course I can. When would you like to reschedule it?

____ 4. Would you please spell your last name for me?

d. I'm sorry. I have an early-morning dentist appointment.

____ 5. Would you mind mailing this letter for me?

e. Sure. It's Djohn@iol.com.

____ 6. Can you cancel tomorrow's meeting for me? I have to go out of town.

f. Sure. . . . Hello, J and R Equities.

____ 7. Will you shut the window, please?

g. Sure. It's M-A-R-D-J-A-I-T.

____ 8. Would you get that box down from the closet?

h. Sorry, but I don't know how. Ask Todd.

____ 9. Could you get the phone for me?

i. I'd like to, but it's too heavy for me to lift.

____ 10. Can you give me Doug Johnson's e-mail address?

j. Not at all.

Write the numbers of the responses that mean "Yes": _2,_____

Write the numbers of the responses that mean "No": _____

Write the number of the response that has a negative word, but means

"OK, I'll do it.": _____

2 | REQUESTS

These conversations take place in an office. Use the correct form of the phrases in the box to complete the requests.

~~answer the phone~~	keep the noise down
buy some stamps	lend me $5.00
come to my office	open the window
explain this note to me	pick up a sandwich
get Frank's phone number	stay late tonight

1. **A:** Could you _____*answer the phone*_____? My hands are full.

   B: Sure. I'll get it.

2. **A:** Would you mind _____? It's really hot in here.

   B: No, not at all.

3. **A:** Can you please _____ for me?

   B: Certainly. I pass the post office on my way home.

4. **A:** I'm going to the coffee shop. Can I get you anything?

   B: Could you _____ for me?

5. **A:** Would you mind _____? We really have to get this

   report done by tomorrow.

   B: I'm sorry, but I have to visit my aunt in the hospital.

6. **A:** Will you _____, please? I can't hear myself think!

   B: Sorry!

7. **A:** Can you _____ when you have the chance?

   B: Sure. I'll be right there.

8. **A:** Would you _____ for me?

   B: It's 555-4345.

9. **A:** Would you mind _____?

   B: Not at all. What don't you understand?

10. **A:** Could you _____?

    B: Oh, I'm sorry. I'm short on cash.

3 | WORD ORDER

Unscramble the words to make requests. Use the correct form of the verbs.

1. come / can / please / here / you

   Can you please come here?

2. work / on Saturday / would you mind

   _____

3. you / me / please / will / help

   _____

4. would / please / explain / you / this

   _____

5. drive / home / you / me / please / could

   _____

4 | EDITING

Read the office notes below and on page 66. There are six mistakes in making requests. The first mistake is already corrected. Find and correct five more. Don't forget to check punctuation.

1.

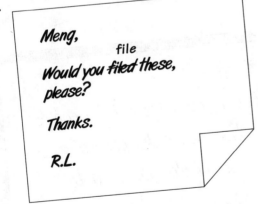

Meng,
                    file
Would you ~~filed~~ these,
please?

Thanks.

R.L.

2.

write it down

Hi Ted,
   Could you please remember to turn off the lights when you leave?
                  Thanks,
                  Lynn

(continued)

3.

HANK,

WILL YOU RETURN PLEASE THE STAPLER?

BRAD

4.

Melida,

Can you make 5 copies of these pages, please?

Thanks,

Ellen

5.

John,

Would you mind leave the finished report on my desk?

Rey

6.

Celia,
Could you please remember to lock the door.
Thank you.

Diana

7.

Annie,
Would you please to call Ms. Rivera before the end of the day?

Thanks,
JF

8.

Todd —
Could you print out 10 copies of the Hendricks report?
Also, would you mind to e-mail Lisa Barker a copy?

Thanks a lot.
Heather

5 | PERSONALIZATION

Write one request that you would like to make of each of the following people.

1. (To your teacher) _____

   _____

2. (To a classmate) _____

   _____

3. (To a friend) _____

   _____

4. (To your boss) _____

   _____

5. (To your landlord) _____

   _____

6. (To _____) _____

   _____

14 Advice: *Should, Ought to, Had better*

1 | AFFIRMATIVE AND NEGATIVE STATEMENTS WITH *SHOULD*

Rewrite these cell-phone tips. Give advice with **should**. *Choose between affirmative and negative.*

CELL-PHONE ETIQUETTE

Cell phones are wonderful, but they can also be very annoying.
Here are some rules you should follow to be polite.

Turn off your cell phone in public places such as movie theaters and class.

1. *You should turn off your cell phone in public places such as movie theaters and class.*

Don't shout into the phone.

2. _____

Speak in a quiet, normal voice.

3. _____

Leave the room to make a phone call.

4. _____

Don't discuss private issues in public places.

5. _____

Don't stand too close to other people when you are talking on the phone.

6. _____

Pay attention to other people on the street when you are walking and talking.

7. _____

Never dial while you are driving.

8. _____

2 | AFFIRMATIVE AND NEGATIVE STATEMENTS WITH *SHOULD, OUGHT TO, HAD BETTER*

Complete these conversations with the correct form of the verbs in parentheses. Choose between affirmative and negative. Use contractions when possible.

1. **A:** Excuse me, but you really _____*shouldn't use*_____ your cell phone in here.
   (should / use)

   The sign says "No cell phones."

   B: Sorry. I didn't see the sign.

2. **A:** You _____ Aunt Rosa. I know she'd be happy to hear from you.
   (should / call)

   B: Good idea. I'll call her as soon as I get off the phone with you.

3. **A:** You _____ to pick up some milk on the way home. We're all out
   (had better / forget)

   of it, and we need it for dinner.

   B: Call me again to remind me. OK?

4. **A:** We _____ the movie at Cinema Village Saturday night. I hear it's
   a. (ought to / see)

   really great.

   B: OK. But we _____ tickets sometime in the afternoon, or it'll be
   b. (had better / buy)

   hard to get in.

5. **A:** We _____ that restaurant near the theater.
   (should / try)

   B: Good idea. I'll call and make a reservation.

6. **A:** Our cell-phone bill is really high. I think we _____ about changing
   a. (ought to / think)

   calling plans.

   B: You're right. We _____ it.
   b. (should / look into)

7. **A:** People really _____ on their cell phones while they're driving. It's
   a. (should / talk)

   really dangerous.

   B: You know, it's illegal in many places.

   A: Well, there _____ a law against it here too.
   b. (should / be)

8. **A:** You _____ Andy now. He's probably already asleep.
   (had better / call)

   B: OK. I'll call him tomorrow.

(continued)

9. **A:** They _____ a "quiet car" on this train. It's hard to work with all
(ought to / have)

these people talking on their cells.

B: That's a great idea.

10. **A:** I _____ call-waiting on my cell phone. I'm missing too many calls.
(should / get)

B: I'm surprised you don't have it already.

11. **A:** I _____ so loud. I think I'm disturbing people around me.
(should / talk)

B: Just call me when you get home. OK?

12. **A:** It's 7:00. I _____ now. I don't want to be late.
(had better / hang up)

B: OK. Talk to you later.

3 | QUESTIONS AND ANSWERS WITH *SHOULD*

Read this invitation. Use the words in parentheses and the information in the invitation to complete the phone conversation.

YOU ARE INVITED TO A PARTY!

FOR: Scott's SURPRISE birthday barbecue

DATE: June 11

TIME: 2:00 P.M. sharp!

PLACE: 20 Greenport Avenue

RSVP by May 15. Please don't call here!
Call Amy's cell phone and leave a message.
500-555-3234.
No gifts, please!
(but please bring something to drink)

LISA: Hi, Tania.

TANIA: Hi, Lisa. What's up?

LISA: Aunt Rosa's having a birthday party for Uncle Scott. She didn't have your new address, so she asked me to call and invite you. It's on June 11. Can you come?

TANIA: Sure. Just give me all the information. (What time / be there)

What time should I be there?
1.

LISA: Let's see. I have the invitation right here.

You should be there at 2:00 P.M. sharp.
                                            2.

TANIA: (What / wear)

_____
                                            3.

LISA: Something casual. It's a barbecue.

TANIA: (bring a gift)

_____
                                            4.

LISA: _____ The invitation says "No gifts."
                     5.

TANIA: OK. What about food? (bring something to eat or drink)

_____
                                            6.

LISA: _____
                                            7.

Oh, and the invitation says "RSVP." In other words, Aunt Rosa wants a response.

TANIA: (When / respond)

_____
                                            8.

LISA: _____
                                            9.

TANIA: (call Aunt Rosa)

_____
                                            10.

LISA: _____ I forgot to tell you. It's a surprise party!
            11.

TANIA: OK. (Who / call)

_____
                                            12.

LISA: _____
                                            13.

TANIA: Fine. Sounds like fun. I'll see you there. Thanks for calling.

LISA: No problem. See you there.

4 | EDITING

*Read this quiz. There are ten mistakes in the use of **should**, **ought to**, and **had better**. The first mistake is already corrected. Find and correct nine more.*

Party Etiquette Quiz

Do you know what you should do at a party? Check the best answer.

1. You are at a party and you can't remember someone's name. What ~~you should~~ *should you* do?

☐ **a.** You should no ask the person's name.

☐ **b.** You better leave immediately!

☐ **c.** You ought just ask.

2. You don't know anyone at the party, and your host doesn't introduce you to the other guests. Had you better introduce yourself?

☐ **a.** Yes, you should. You should say, "Hi. My name's _____."

☐ **b.** No, you should. You'd better tell the host to introduce you.

3. Your cell phone rings during the party. You should answer it?

☐ **a.** Just let it ring. You had not better answer it.

☐ **b.** You should answer it, but just have a short conversation.

☐ **c.** You really ought to leave the room and speak to the person in private.

4. You had a very nice time at the party. How you should thank your host?

☐ **a.** You should just say "thank you" when you leave.

☐ **b.** You should send a "thank you" e-mail the next day.

☐ **c.** You oughta write a long "thank you" letter and send a gift too.

5 | PERSONALIZATION

A friend of yours is going to a party. He or she won't know anyone there and feels a little nervous. Write five sentences giving your friend advice. Use your own paper.

Suggestions: *Let's, Could, Why don't , Why not, How about*

1 | SUGGESTIONS

Match the two halves of each suggestion. Notice the end punctuation—period (.) or question mark (?).

___c___ 1. My feet hurt. Why don't we

_____ 2. The weather's terrible. How about

_____ 3. We have an hour before the show starts. We could

_____ 4. You look exhausted. Why don't I

_____ 5. This concert is terrible. Let's not

_____ 6. I'm really hungry. How about

_____ 7. There's so much to see! How about

_____ 8. If John's unhappy at the Blue Water Inn, why doesn't he

_____ 9. It's going to be hot tomorrow. Let's

_____ 10. There's a gift shop. Maybe we could

a. going to a movie?

b. have a cup of coffee.

c. take a taxi?

d. go to the beach.

e. getting a slice of pizza?

f. change hotels?

g. meet you back at the hotel?

h. buy some souvenirs there.

i. taking a walking tour?

j. stay until the end.

2 | PUNCTUATION

Circle the correct phrase to complete these conversations between tourists on vacation. Add the correct punctuation: period (.) or question mark (?).

1. **A:** I'm exhausted. We've been walking for hours.

   B: How about / (Why don't we) sit on that bench for a while _?_

2. **A:** I'm almost out of film.

   B: There's a drugstore over there. Maybe you could / Let's not get film there __

(continued)

3. **A:** It would be nice to see some of the countryside.

   B: <u>Let's / How about</u> rent a car ___

4. **A:** <u>Why not / How about</u> taking a bus tour ___

   B: That's a good idea. It's less expensive than renting a car.

5. **A:** I want to take a picture of that building. <u>Why don't you / How about</u> stand in front of it ___

   B: OK.

6. **A:** We have an hour before we have to meet the rest of our tour group.

   B: <u>Let's / Let's not</u> get a cup of coffee in that café ___

   A: Good idea. I could use something to drink.

7. **A:** I heard it's going to rain tomorrow.

   B: <u>Maybe we could / How about</u> go to a museum ___

8. **A:** You know, Sara really enjoys going to museums.

   B: <u>Why don't / Why doesn't</u> she come with us ___

9. **A:** I really need to get a better map of the city.

   B: <u>Why don't you / Let's not</u> stop at that tourist information office ___

   I'm sure they have maps.

10. **A:** I don't know what to get for my daughter.

    B: <u>Why don't you / How about</u> getting one of those sweatshirts ___

11. **A:** I'm tired, and my feet are starting to hurt.

    B: <u>Maybe we could / How about</u> sit on one of those benches over there ___

12. **A:** Look at that beautiful building. Why don't you take a picture of it?

    B: <u>That's a good idea / Because I don't want to</u> ___

3 | SUGGESTIONS

Look at the tourist flyer. Use the suggestions in the flyer to complete the conversation.

BOSTON Highlights

Here are some of the many things you can do in this "capital of New England":

☐ **Go to Haymarket**—open-air fruit and vegetable stands (Fridays and Saturdays only).

☑ **Visit Faneuil Hall Marketplace**—restoration of Boston's historic Quincy Market. Shops, restaurants.

☐ **Go to the New England Aquarium**—412 species, 7,606 specimens.

☐ **Walk along the waterfront**—offices, shops, parks for picnics.

☐ **Take the "T"**—Boston's subway system.

☐ **Take a boat excursion**—cruise the harbor and Massachusetts Bay (1½ hours).

☐ **Go shopping in Downtown Crossing**—Boston's pedestrian zone.

☐ **Take an elevator to the top of the John Hancock Observatory**—the tallest building in New England.

☐ **Walk the Freedom Trail**—1½ miles of historic points of interest.

☐ **Eat at Legal Sea Foods**—restaurant chain famous for fresh fish at reasonable prices.

A: Wow, there's so much to do! I don't know where to begin!

B: Why don't we _____ *visit Faneuil Hall Marketplace* _____? We can have
1.
breakfast there and then do some shopping.

A: Sounds good. How will we get there?

B: Let's _____. I always like to see what
2.
the public transportation is like.

A: OK. After that, maybe we could _____
3.
and pick up some fresh fruit for later on. It's right across from there.

(continued)

B: We can't. It's only open Fridays and Saturdays.

A: Oh, too bad. How about _____ ?
4.

We could get a "bird's-eye" view of the city that way.

B: I don't know. I'm a little afraid of heights. But I've got another idea. Why don't we

_____ ? That way we could still see a
5.

lot of the city.

A: That sounds like a good idea. It'll be nice being on the water. And afterwards, how about

_____ ? I hear they have the largest
6.

glass-enclosed saltwater tank in the world.

B: Speaking of fish, why don't we _____
7.

tonight?

A: Good idea. But we should make a reservation. It's a very popular place.

B: So, we've decided what to do for breakfast and dinner. What about lunch?

A: Maybe we could _____ and have a
8.

picnic in the park.

B: And then, how about _____ ? I need to
9.

buy some souvenirs, and we won't have to worry about traffic. It's a pedestrian zone.

A: I don't know. Why don't we _____ ?
10.

I'd really like to see some more historic sights. We can look for souvenirs tomorrow.

4 | PERSONALIZATION

Imagine you are in Boston with a friend. Look at the flyer in Exercise 3. Complete these suggestions to your friend.

1. Why don't we _____

2. How about _____

3. Let's _____

4. Maybe we could _____

5. But let's not _____

Present Perfect:
Since and *For*

1 | SPELLING: REGULAR AND IRREGULAR VERBS

Write the past participles.

Base Form	Simple Past	Past Participle
1. be	was/were	*been*
2. bring	brought	_____
3. come	came	_____
4. eat	ate	_____
5. fall	fell	_____
6. get	got	_____
7. have	had	_____
8. look	looked	_____
9. lose	lost	_____
10. play	played	_____
11. watch	watched	_____
12. win	won	_____

2 | *SINCE* OR *FOR*

*Complete these sentences with **since** or **for**.*

1. I haven't known Ana ____*for*____ a long time.

2. She has been on my soccer team only _____ last September.

3. We've become good friends _____ then.

4. Our team hasn't been in a game _____ a few weeks.

5. _____ our last game, we've practiced a lot.

(continued)

6. _____ weeks we've gone to the field every day after class.

7. We haven't lost a game _____ several months.

8. I have loved sports _____ I was a little girl.

3 | AFFIRMATIVE STATEMENTS WITH *SINCE* AND *FOR*

Complete these biographies of two athletes who have been famous since they were children. Use the present perfect form of the verbs in parentheses and choose between **since** *and* **for**.

Biography A

Tiger Woods (1976–   ) When Tiger Woods was only 18 months old, his father gave him a sawed-off golf club. Woods ___has loved___

1. (love)

the game of golf _____ then. As a teenager, he won
2. (since / for)

many amateur titles. At 16 he was the youngest person to play in a

professional golf tournament.

_____ then, he _____ to win many
3. (Since / For)   4. (go on)

major tournaments and to break many records. _____ the past few years, TV
5. (Since / For)

viewers _____ him in many commercials. _____ he turned
6. (see)   7. (Since / For)

professional, Woods _____ more money and _____ more records
8. (earn)   9. (break)

at a younger age than any other golfer.

Biography B

Michelle Kwan (1980–   ) Michelle Kwan _____ at
1. (be)

home on the ice _____ most of her life. She started
2. (since / for)

skating when she was five and won her first skating competition a

year later. _____ that time, Kwan _____
3. (Since / For)   4. (win)

more competitions—including five Worlds—than almost any other

skater, and she _____ one of the most famous figure
5. (become)

skaters in the world. Her trophies include silver and bronze Olympic

medals, but not the gold—the prize she _____ of _____ she was a
6. (dream)   7. (since / for)

little girl. _____ her last disappointment at the Olympics, Kwan _____
8. (Since / For)   9. (continue)

skating, winning major competitions and thrilling audiences with her skill and grace.

4 | QUESTIONS AND ANSWERS

Use the words in parentheses to write questions about the athletes in Exercise 3. Look at the information again and answer the questions.

1. (How long / Tiger Woods / love golf)

   A: *How long has Tiger Woods loved golf?*

   B: *He has loved golf since he was 18 months old* OR *for more than 25 years.*

2. (How long / he / be a professional golfer)

   A: _____

   B: _____

3. (he / win any major tournaments since he turned professional)

   A: _____

   B: _____

4. (How long / he / be in TV commercials)

   A: _____

   B: _____

5. (How long / Michelle Kwan / be a skater)

   A: _____

   B: _____

6. (How many World Competitions / she / win since 1986)

   A: _____

   B: _____

7. (she / get an Olympic gold medal since she began competing)

   A: _____

   B: _____

8. (she / skate again since the Olympics)

   A: _____

   B: _____

5 | AFFIRMATIVE AND NEGATIVE STATEMENTS

Read each pair of sentences. Use the correct present perfect form to complete or write a summary sentence that has a meaning similar to the two sentences.

1. **a.** Tanya and Boris became skaters in 1998.

    b. They are still skaters.

    SUMMARY: *Tanya and Boris have been skaters* _____ since 1998.

2. **a.** Fei-Mei and Natasha competed in 1992.

    b. That was the last time they competed.

    SUMMARY: *Fei-Mei and Natasha haven't competed since 1992.* _____

3. **a.** Min Ho won two awards in 1998.

    b. He won another award in 1999.

    SUMMARY: _____ since 1998.

4. **a.** Marilyn entered a competition in 1998.

    b. She entered another competition last year.

    SUMMARY: _____ since 1998.

5. **a.** Victor and Marilyn saw each other in 1998.

    b. That was the last time they saw each other.

    SUMMARY: _____

6. **a.** Karl became a golfer in 1999.

    b. He is still a golfer.

    SUMMARY: _____

7. **a.** Karl lost two tournaments in February of this year.

    b. He lost another tournament last week.

    SUMMARY: _____ since February of this year.

8. **a.** Andreas went to a tennis match two years ago.

    b. That was the last match he went to.

    SUMMARY: _____ for two years.

Present Perfect: Already and Yet

1 | SPELLING: REGULAR AND IRREGULAR VERBS

Write the past participles.

Base Form	Simple Past	Past Participle
1. act	acted	*acted*
2. become	became	_____
3. dance	danced	_____
4. drink	drank	_____
5. fight	fought	_____
6. give	gave	_____
7. hold	held	_____
8. keep	kept	_____
9. know	knew	_____
10. sing	sang	_____
11. smile	smiled	_____
12. travel	traveled	_____

2 | QUESTIONS AND STATEMENTS WITH *ALREADY* AND *YET*

*Complete this conversation with the correct form of the verbs in parentheses and **already** or **yet**. Choose between affirmative and negative. Use contractions if possible.*

TED: I hear you're looking for a new apartment. _____*Have*_____ you

_____*found*_____ one _____*yet*_____?

1. (find)

MIA: No. And we're getting discouraged. We _____ at more than 10, and

2. (look)

we _____ one that we like _____!

3. (find)

(continued)

TED: Well, don't give up. I _____ at least 20. Are you working with a

   _{4. (see)}

real estate agent?

MIA: No. We wanted to try to find something ourselves, so we _____ to

   _{5. (go)}

an agent _____. But I think we may need to. Unfortunately, we

_____ a lot of time looking at apartments that were completely

   _{6. (waste)}

wrong for us.

TED: I know what you mean. _____ you _____

   _{7. (decide)}

on a neighborhood _____?

MIA: No. We _____ our minds _____. What

   _{8. (make up)}

about you?

TED: We'd really like to stay in this neighborhood. We just need a bigger place.

3 | QUESTIONS AND STATEMENTS WITH *ALREADY* AND *YET*

*Mia is going to move. Read her list of things to do. She has checked (✔) all the things she's
already done. Write questions and answers about the words in parentheses.*

Moving Checklist

- ☑ choose a moving company
- ☐ find a painter
- ☑ collect boxes for packing
- ☑ get a change-of-address form from the post office
- ☐ begin to pack clothes
- ☑ make a list of cleaning supplies
- ☐ clean the refrigerator and stove
- ☑ buy two bookcases
- ☑ give away the old couch
- ☐ buy a new couch
- ☐ throw away old magazines
- ☐ invite the neighbors over for a good-bye party

1. **A:** (moving company) *Has she chosen a moving company yet?*

   B: *Yes, she's already chosen a moving company.*

2. **A:** (clothes) *Has she begun to pack clothes yet?*

   B: *No, she hasn't begun to pack clothes yet.*

3. **A:** (bookcases) _____

   B: _____

4. **A:** (magazines) _____

   B: _____

5. **A:** (painter) _____

   B: _____

6. **A:** (boxes) _____

   B: _____

7. **A:** (new couch) _____

   B: _____

8. **A:** (old couch) _____

   B: _____

9. **A:** (refrigerator and stove) _____

   B: _____

10. **A:** (cleaning supplies) _____

    B: _____

11. **A:** (change-of-address form) _____

    B: _____

12. **A:** (the neighbors) _____

    B: _____

4 | EDITING

*Mia sent an e-mail to her friend. There are six mistakes in the use of the present perfect with **already** and **yet**. The first one is already corrected. Find and correct five more.*

Hi,

> I'm writing to you from our new apartment! We've already ~~be~~ *been* here two weeks, and we feel very much at home. But there's still a lot to do. Believe it or not, we haven't unpacked all the boxes already! We took most of our old furniture, so we don't need to get too much new stuff. We had to buy a new couch for the living room, but they haven't delivered it yet.

> We've already meet some of our new neighbors. They seem very nice. One of them have already invited us over for coffee.

> Had you made vacation plans yet? As soon as we get the couch (it's a sleeper), we'd love for you to visit. Already we've planned places to take you when you come!

> —Mia

Present Perfect: Indefinite Past

1 | SPELLING: REGULAR AND IRREGULAR VERBS

Write the past participles.

Base Form	Simple Past	Past Participle
1. begin	began	*begun*
2. decide	decided	_____
3. fly	flew	_____
4. go	went	_____
5. hear	heard	_____
6. keep	kept	_____
7. make	made	_____
8. ride	rode	_____
9. see	saw	_____
10. swim	swam	_____
11. travel	traveled	_____
12. work	worked	_____

2 | AFFIRMATIVE STATEMENTS

Complete these statements. Use the present perfect form of the correct verbs from Exercise 1.

1. Julie _____ *has made* _____ several trips this year.

2. You _____ on a camel. Did you enjoy it?

3. I'd like to go to Costa Rica. I _____ that it's beautiful.

4. They _____ the Pyramids before.

5. He _____ Air France many times. It's his favorite airline.

(continued)

6. I _____ with dolphins in the ocean. What an adventure!

7. My cousin _____ to go hiking in northern Spain next fall.

8. She _____ hard this year and really needs a vacation.

3 | AFFIRMATIVE AND NEGATIVE STATEMENTS

Read this article about a famous series of travel guides. Complete the sentences with the present perfect form of the verbs in parentheses.

As you probably know, travel _____*has become*_____ very, very popular. As a result,
                 1. (become)

hundreds of travel guides _____ on bookstore shelves. One of the most
            2. (appear)

popular travel-guide series is *Lonely Planet*. It began in the early 1970s by Tony and Maureen

Wheeler. The husband-and-wife team _____ always really

_____ traveling, and they _____. They still make
    3. (love)   **4. (not stop)**

a lot of trips all over the world. The first *Lonely Planet* guidebook was the result of one of their

first trips. Today the series has more than 650 guidebooks, and Tony Wheeler

_____ and _____ to more than 20 of them. The
    5. (write)   **6. (contribute)**

Wheelers _____ both _____ awards for their
                        7. (receive)

work, and *The New York Times* _____ Tony as "the most influential man
              8. (describe)

in travel."

    Recently, *Lonely Planet* _____ a new edition of all their books. The
                9. (introduce)

publisher _____ almost 4,000 new maps and 23,000 new pages. Tony
      10. (include)

Wheeler says this "re-launch" _____ them a real opportunity to improve
              11. (give)

the series. The huge project _____ easy, but according to publisher Simon
          12. (not be)

Westcott, it _____ worth the effort. "We're really proud of what we
        13. (be)

_____," he said. "We _____ the best guidebooks
    14. (do)   **15. (produce)**

a traveler can buy."

    Lonely Planet books are quite different from other guidebooks. The travel series

_____ always _____ travelers to do and explore
                16. (encourage)

new things—not just the "Top-Ten Tourist Sights." If you _____ a *Lonely*
                  17. (not read)

Planet guide, check one out. We promise you: It will be an adventure—even if you never leave

your armchair!

4 | QUESTIONS AND ANSWERS WITH ADVERBS AND TIME EXPRESSIONS

A travel agent is talking to a client. Complete the travel agent's questions with the words in parentheses. Use the agent's notes and the correct adverb or time expression from the box to answer the questions. You will use some words more than once.

many times	never	not lately	once	recently	twice

Adventure Travel Inc.

Egypt — 2 X
Europe — more than 10 X
African safari — (returned two months ago)
Costa Rica — 1 X (1999)
China — no

hot-air ballooning — no
dolphin swim — 6 X or more

group tour — no (and <u>not</u> interested)

1. **AGENT:** _Have you ever been_ _____ to Egypt?
   (ever / be)
   CLIENT: _I've been to Egypt twice._ _____

2. **AGENT:** _____ Europe?
   (How many times / visit)
   CLIENT: _____

3. **AGENT:** _____ on an African safari?
   (ever / be)
   CLIENT: _____

4. **AGENT:** _____ to Costa Rica?
   (ever / be)
   CLIENT: _____

5. **AGENT:** _____ there?
   (How often / be)
   CLIENT: _____

(continued)

6. AGENT: _____ in China?
   (travel)

   CLIENT: _____

7. AGENT: _____ in a hot-air balloon?
   (ever / go up)

   CLIENT: _____

8. AGENT: _____ with dolphins?
   (ever / swim)

   CLIENT: _____

9. AGENT: _____ a group tour?
   (ever / take)

   CLIENT: _____ . And I never want to!

5 | PERSONALIZATION

Write sentences about your own travel experience. Use the present perfect with adverbs or
time expressions like **never**, **twice**, **recently**, **not lately**, *and* **many times**.

1. _____

2. _____

3. _____

4. _____

5. _____

6. _____

Present Perfect and Simple Past

1 | PRESENT PERFECT OR SIMPLE PAST

Complete the sentences about Tom Dorsey, a teacher who is looking for a job in another city.

Last Year

1. Tom answered 20 employment ads.

2. _____Tom had_____ two job interviews.

3. Tom went on one out-of-town interview.

4. _____ one job offer.

5. Tom made $30,000.

6. _____ a lot of interesting people.

7. Tom was sick once.

8. _____ well.

9. _____ a new camera.

10. Tom paid with cash.

11. Tom read five books.

12. Tom didn't take a vacation.

13. Tom didn't give any parties.

14. _____ discouraged.

This Year

_____Tom has answered_____ 30 ads.

Tom has had three job interviews.

_____ on two out-of-town interviews.

Tom has gotten three job offers.

_____ the same amount of money.

Tom has met a lot of interesting people too.

_____ sick twice.

Tom has looked tired.

Tom has bought a DVD player.

_____ by credit card.

_____ two books.

_____ a vacation. He went to Florida.

_____ two parties.

Tom has felt more encouraged.

2 | PRESENT PERFECT OR SIMPLE PAST

A journalist is interviewing a woman about marriage. Complete the interview with the correct form of the verbs in parentheses. Use the present perfect or the simple past.

INTERVIEWER: How long _____ *have* _____ you _____ *been* _____ married?
1. (be)

WOMAN: We _____ married in 2001, so we _____ married for
2. (get)   3. (be)
just a few years.

INTERVIEWER: And when _____ you _____ your first child?
4. (have)

WOMAN: Well, I _____ a mother pretty quickly. We _____
5. (become)   6. (have)
Stephanie 10 months after we _____ married.
7. (be)

INTERVIEWER: You say this isn't your first marriage. How long _____ your first

marriage _____?
8. (last)

WOMAN: About two years. We _____ in 1998.
9. (divorce)

INTERVIEWER: _____ the two of you _____ any kids?
10. (have)

WOMAN: No, we _____.
11.

INTERVIEWER: Do you still see your first husband?

WOMAN: Yes. We _____ friends. In fact, I _____ him last week.
12. (remain)   13. (see)
He and Tom _____ friends too.
14. (become)

INTERVIEWER: _____ he _____?
15. (remarry)

WOMAN: No, he _____.
16.

INTERVIEWER: In your opinion, why _____ your first marriage _____?
17. (fail)

WOMAN: I think that we _____ married too young. We _____
18. (get)   19. (not know)
each other well enough.

INTERVIEWER: Where _____ you _____ Tom?
20. (meet)

WOMAN: In Atlanta. We _____ both students there.
21. (be)

INTERVIEWER: And when _____ you _____ to Los Angeles?
22. (move)

WOMAN: Last year. Los Angeles is the third city we _____ in! Tom is a college
23. (live)
professor, and it's hard to find a permanent job these days.

3 | PRESENT PERFECT OR SIMPLE PAST

Read some facts about the changing American family. Complete the sentences with the present perfect or simple past form of the verbs in the boxes.

begin	~~change~~	get	have

The American family ___*has changed*___ a lot in the past 45 years. In the 1960s, couples
1.
_____ to get married at an older age. They also _____ divorced more
2.   3.
frequently than they ever did, and they _____ fewer children.
4.

be	create	occur	rise

Age

In 1960, the average age for marriage for women _____ 20.3 and for men,
5.
22.8. Today it _____ to 25.1 for women and 26.8 for men. In the early 1960s, most
6.
divorces _____ among couples older than 45. Today people of all ages are getting
7.
divorced at a very high rate. This, in part, _____ many single-parent homes.
8.

be	have	increase	start

Birth Rate

In the mid-1960s, birth rates _____ to drop. Then, almost 60 percent of women
9.
_____ three or more children by the time they _____ in their late 30s.
10.   11.
These days, 35 percent of women in the same age group have only two children. In addition, the

number of births to older women _____ greatly _____.
12.

change	get	reach	stay

Living Arrangements

Before 1960, most children _____ in their parents' homes until they
13.
_____ married. This pattern _____ since then. Today many single
14.   15.

(continued)

people live alone. Also affecting today's living arrangements is the fact that life expectancy

_____ an all-time high of 77.6 years. This means that there are a lot more older

     16.

people, and some of them are moving in with their adult children.

4 | EDITING

Read this student's e-mail to a friend. There are eight mistakes in the use of the present perfect and the simple past. The first mistake is already corrected. Find and correct seven more.

Hi, Jennifer—

                    met

Last month, I ~~have met~~ the most wonderful guy. His name is Roger, and he is a

student in my night class. He lived here since 1992. Before that he lived in Detroit

too, so we have a lot in common. Roger has been married for five years but got

divorced last April.

Roger and I spent a lot of time together. Last week I saw him every night, and this

week we already gotten together three times after class. Monday night we have

seen a great movie. Did you see *The Purple Room*? It's playing at all the theaters.

We've decided to take a trip back to Detroit in the summer. Maybe we can get

together. It would be great to see you again. Please let me know if you'll be there.

                        Love,

                        Diana

Here's a photo of Roger that I've taken a few weeks ago.

---

5 | PERSONALIZATION

Complete these sentences with information about your own life.

1. This year, _____

2. Last year, _____

3. _____ since 2000.

4. Four years ago, _____

5. For the past two years, _____

20 Present Perfect Progressive and Present Perfect

1 | PRESENT PERFECT PROGRESSIVE STATEMENTS

Read the information about Amanda and Pete Kelly. Write a sentence—affirmative or negative—that summarizes the information. Use the present perfect progressive with **since** *or* **for**.

1. It's 9:00. Amanda began working at 7:00. She is still working.

   Amanda has been working since 7:00 OR *for two hours.*

2. She is writing articles about elephants. She began a series last month.

   _____

3. Amanda and Pete used to live in New York. They left New York a few years ago.

   _____

4. They are now living in London. They moved there in 2004.

   _____

5. Pete was selling books. He stopped last year.

   _____

6. Pete and Amanda are thinking of opening their own business. They began thinking about this last year.

   _____

7. Pete went back to school last month. He's studying economics.

   _____

8. Amanda and Pete started looking for a new apartment a month ago. They're still looking.

   _____

2 | PRESENT PERFECT PROGRESSIVE OR PRESENT PERFECT

Read this article about a famous British businesswoman and environmentalist. Complete the information with the present perfect progressive or present perfect form of the verbs in parentheses. If both forms are possible, use the present perfect progressive.

Born in 1942, the child of an Italian immigrant family living in England, Anita Roddick _____*has become*_____ one of the
1. (become)
most successful businesswomen in the world. Today she is the owner of an international chain of stores that sells soaps, makeup, body lotions, and creams. For more than 25 years, The Body Shop

_____ products that are "environmentally
2. (sell)
friendly." They are made mostly of natural products from renewable sources, and they come in biodegradable, recyclable containers. In addition, Roddick, who _____
3. (fight)
for years against the practice of animal testing of cosmetics, refuses to use any animals to test her products.

The first Body Shop opened in Brighton, England, in 1976. Since then, more than 2,000 stores in 50 countries around the world _____.
4. (open)
Roddick relies on the reputation of her products and stores to attract customers. She

_____ never _____ much advertising for her
5. (do)
stores. Word of mouth _____ her chief way of getting new customers.
6. (be)
Roddick spends much of her time traveling. Right now she is "on the road." For the past several months, she _____ around the world in search of new ideas for
7. (travel)
her body-care products.

Roddick is more than a businesswoman. She _____ several awards,
8. (receive)
including the United Nations Global 500 environmental award. She is also concerned with human rights. Lately, she _____ hard to improve the earnings of workers who
9. (work)
make clothes for large multinational stores.

(continued)

Roddick _____ several books. Her latest one, *Business as Unusual:*
$\qquad$ **10. (write)**

My Entrepreneurial Journey, tells how Roddick _____ successfully

_____ business with social responsibility. She hopes her story will serve as
$\qquad$ **11. (combine)**

a model to other people. According to one writer for *Inc.*, a business magazine, it already has:

"This woman _____ business forever," wrote Bo Burlingham in 1990.
$\qquad$ **12. (change)**

More than 15 years later, Roddick continues to be a force for change in both the business and

social worlds.

3 | PRESENT PERFECT PROGRESSIVE OR PRESENT PERFECT

Complete this conversation between two friends. Use the present perfect progressive or present perfect form of the verbs in parentheses.

A: Hi. I _____*haven't seen*_____ you around lately. How _____
$\qquad$ **1. (not see)**

 you _____?
$\qquad$ **2. (be)**

B: OK, thanks. What about you?

A: Not bad. What _____ you _____?
$\qquad$ **3. (do)**

B: Nothing special. What about you?

A: I _____ a book for this business course I'm taking. It's called *Business*
$\qquad$ **4. (read)**

 as Unusual. It's pretty interesting.

B: Who wrote it?

A: Anita Roddick. _____ you ever _____
$\qquad$ **5. (read)**

 anything about her?

B: Yes. I _____ a few articles about her in the paper.
$\qquad$ **6. (see)**

A: _____ you ever _____ any of her products?
$\qquad$ **7. (buy)**

B: As a matter of fact, I _____ her products for years.
$\qquad$ **8. (use)**

A: Oh. Where do you buy them?

B: I used to go downtown, but a new Body Shop _____ just

_____ on Broadway.
$\qquad$ **9. (open)**

A: Wow, they _____ everywhere, haven't they? I wonder where the next
$\qquad$ **10. (open)**

 one is going to be.

4 | QUESTIONS: PRESENT PERFECT PROGRESSIVE OR PRESENT PERFECT

Write questions about Anita Roddick. Use the words in parentheses and the present perfect progressive or present perfect.

1. (she / sell / body products for a long time)

   Has she been selling body products for a long time?

2. (How long / she / be / a businesswoman)

   _____

3. (How much money / her business / make this year)

   _____

4. (How long / she / travel around the world)

   _____

5. (How many countries / she / visit)

   _____

6. (her shops / open / in Asia)

   _____

7. (How many copies of her book / she / sell)

   _____

8. (she / write / any books since *Business as Unusual*)

   _____

9. (How many awards / she / receive)

   _____

10. (What / she / work on / these days)

   _____

11. (How long / she and her husband / live in England)

   _____

5 | EDITING

Read this journal entry. There are seven mistakes in the use of the present perfect progressive and present perfect. The first mistake is already corrected. Find and correct six more.

Friday, Sept. 15

been taking
It's the second week of the fall semester. I've ~~taken~~ a business course with Professor McCarthy. For the past two weeks, we've studying people who have been becoming very successful in the world of business. As part of the course, we've been reading books by or about internationally famous businesspeople.

For example, I've just been finishing a book by Bill Gates, the CEO of Microsoft, called Business @ the Speed of Thought. It was fascinating. Since then, I've read Business as Unusual by Anita Roddick, the owner of The Body Shop. I've only been reading about 50 pages of the book so far, but it seems interesting. Although I bought her products ever since one of her stores opened in my neighborhood, I really didn't know much about her.

Workbook Answer Key

In this answer key, where the contracted form is given, the full form is often also correct, and where the full form is given, the contracted form is often also correct.

UNIT 1 (pages 1–8)

1

2. getting, gets
3. giving, gives
4. grabbing, grabs
5. having, has
6. planning, plans
7. saying, says
8. starting, starts
9. trying, tries
10. watching, watches

2

2. drives
3. takes
4. isn't taking
5. 's taking
6. are repairing
7. is using
8. doesn't . . . use
9. takes
10. moves
11. is slowing down
12. 's raining
13. doesn't like
14. drives
15. is listening
16. listens
17. is describing
18. isn't moving
19. hates
20. doesn't want
21. feels
22. knows
23. is

3

Answers will vary.

4

Postcard A

2. 'm standing
3. is getting
4. looks
5. rains
6. has
7. 's taking
8. 's starting

Postcard B

1. love
2. 'm studying
3. living
4. is improving
5. speak
6. 're helping
7. want
8. miss

5

3. Aldo and Emilia (OR They) go to school.
4. Aldo and Emilia (OR They) are having lunch.
5. Aldo works at the bookstore. Emilia studies at the library.
6. Aldo plays soccer. Emilia plays basketball.
7. Aldo is going home. Emilia is doing homework at the library.
8. Aldo has dinner. Emilia practices the guitar.
9. Aldo does homework. Emilia has dinner.
10. Aldo is playing computer games. Emilia is watching TV.

6

2. Aldo doesn't watch TV. He reads the newspaper.
3. Emilia doesn't work at the bookstore. Aldo works at the bookstore. (OR She studies at the library.)
4. Emilia isn't playing tennis. She's playing basketball.
5. They don't always have dinner together. Aldo has dinner at 6:00. Emilia has dinner at 7:00.

7

2. A: When do Aldo and Emilia get up?
   B: They get up at 7:30.
3. A: Does Emilia walk in the morning?
   B: No, she doesn't.
4. A: What are they doing now?
   B: They're having lunch.
5. A: Is Aldo doing homework now?
   B: No, he isn't.
6. A: Does Emilia do her homework at school?
   B: No, she doesn't.
7. A: When does Emilia play basketball?
   B: (She plays basketball) At 4:00.
8. A: Does Aldo play computer games before dinner?
   B: No, he doesn't.

8

2. Emilia is usually on time.
3. Aldo and Emilia never miss school.
4. These days they're studying English. OR They're studying English these days.
5. They usually speak Italian.
6. Now they're speaking English. OR They're speaking English now.
7. Aldo and Emilia always do their homework.
8. Aldo is often tired.
9. The students usually eat lunch in school.
10. They're always hungry.
11. At the moment Emilia is having a snack. OR Emilia is having a snack at the moment.
12. Emilia rarely goes to bed late.

9

    How are you? ~~I write~~ *I'm writing* you this e-mail before my class.

    I ~~am having~~ *have* a part-time job as a clerk in the mail room of a small company. The pay isn't good, but ~~I'm liking~~ *I like* the people there. They're all friendly, and we ~~are speaking~~ *speak* Spanish all the time. I'm also taking Spanish classes at night at a language institute. The class ~~is meeting~~ *meets* three times a week. It just started last week, so ~~I'm not knowing~~ *I don't know* many of the other students yet. They seem nice, though.

    ~~I'm thinking~~ *I think* that I'm beginning to get accustomed to living here. At first I experienced some "culture shock." I understand that this is quite normal. But these days ~~I meet~~ *I'm meeting* more and more people because of my job and my class, so I'm feeling more connected to things.

    What ~~do you do~~ *are you doing* these days? ~~Do you still look~~ *Are you still looking* for a new job?

    Please write when you can. ~~I'm always liking~~ *I always like* to hear from you.

10

Answers will vary.

UNIT 2 (pages 9–11)

1

3. Don't lean backward.
4. Take a small step.
5. Don't breathe in.
6. Count slowly.
7. Don't speak loudly.
8. Keep your eyes shut.
9. Don't wear tight clothes.
10. Wear a white T-shirt.
11. Wear light clothes.
12. Don't turn the lights off.
13. Turn the music up.
14. Put the heat on low.
15. Don't come late.
16. Don't lock the bottom lock.

2

3. Walk	10. Continue
4. ride	11. stop
5. Show	12. Don't cross
6. Give	13. be
7. Go	14. Don't pass
8. Don't turn	15. Have
9. make	16. Don't work

3

Your mother called. ~~Calls~~ *Call* her at your sister's tonight.
Don't ~~you~~ call after 10:00, though.
I went to the gym.

Please wash*
~~Wash please~~ the dishes and ~~threw~~ *throw* out the trash.
^
If anyone calls for me, ~~takes~~ *take* a message.

Thanks a lot and ~~has~~ *have* a good evening!

*OTHER POSSIBLE CORRECTIONS: Wash the dishes, please, and throw out the trash. OR Wash the dishes and throw out the trash, please.

4

Answers will vary.

UNIT 3 (pages 12–18)

1

2. began	17. met
3. bought	18. moved
4. caught	19. needed
5. came	20. opened
6. died	21. put
7. did	22. read
8. felt	23. said
9. found	24. saw
10. got	25. took
11. gave	26. thought
12. had	27. understood
13. hurried	28. voted
14. kissed	29. won
15. lived	30. wrote
16. looked	31. was, were

2

2. was	7. was, wasn't
3. weren't, were	8. wasn't, was
4. wasn't	9. were
5. was	10. were
6. wasn't, was	

3

2. A: Where was Simone de Beauvoir from?
   B: She was from France.
3. A: What nationality was Pablo Neruda?
   B: He was Chilean.
4. A: Who was Boccaccio?
   B: He was a poet and storyteller.
5. A: Was Agatha Christie French?
   B: No, she wasn't.
6. A: What nationality was Lucy M. Montgomery?
   B: She was Canadian.
7. A: Was Nazim Hikmet a poet?
   B: Yes, he was.
8. A: When was Karel Čapek born?
   B: He was born in 1890.
9. A: Who was Isaak Babel?
   B: He was a short-story writer and playwright.

4

Biography A

2. grew up	6. used
3. taught	7. wrote
4. began	8. moved
5. loved	9. died

Biography B

1. was	6. taught
2. planned	7. loved
3. began	8. married
4. painted	9. had
5. studied	10. died

Biography C

1. were	4. watched
2. built	5. took place
3. flew	6. lasted

5

2. A: Where did he grow up?
   B: He grew up in Hungary.
3. A: What did he do?
   B: He was a composer. OR He wrote music.
4. A: Did he spend his whole life in Hungary?
   B: No, he didn't.
5. A: Did Frida Kahlo plan to be a painter?
   B: No, she didn't.
6. A: When did she begin painting?
   B: She began painting after a serious accident.
7. A: What did she paint?
   B: She painted pictures of her family and friends. She also painted pictures of herself.
8. A: When did she die?
   B: She died in 1954.
9. A: Where did the Wright brothers build their first planes?
   B: (They built their first planes) in their bicycle shop in Ohio.
10. A: Did both brothers fly the *Flyer 1*?
    B: No, they didn't.
11. A: Where did the first controlled flight take place?
    B: (It took place) near Kitty Hawk, North Carolina.
12. A: How long did the flight last?
    B: (It lasted) only about 12 seconds.

6

3. Orville didn't have serious health problems.
4. Wilbur didn't grow a moustache.
5. Orville didn't lose most of his hair.
6. Wilbur didn't take courses in Latin.
7. Wilbur didn't like to play jokes.
8. Wilbur didn't dress very fashionably.
9. Wilbur didn't play the guitar.
10. Orville didn't build the first glider.
11. Orville didn't make the first attempts to fly.
12. Orville didn't choose the location of Kitty Hawk.
13. Wilbur didn't have a lot of patience.
14. Wilbur didn't live a long life.

7

Pablo Neruda (1904–1973) ~~were~~ *was* a famous poet, political activist, and diplomat. He was born in Parral, Chile. When he was 17 he ~~gone~~ *went* to Santiago to continue his education. He did not ~~finished~~ *finish*, but he soon published his first book. Neruda ~~spends~~ *spent* the next several decades traveling and continuing to write poetry. In 1971, while he was Chile's ambassador to France, he ~~winned~~ *won* the Nobel Prize in literature. He ~~dead~~ *died* two years later.

UNIT 4 (pages 19–23)

1

2. wasn't writing
3. was answering
4. were eating
5. weren't eating
6. was attending
7. weren't writing
8. were discussing
9. wasn't answering
10. was returning

2

2. A: What was he doing at 9:30?
   B: He was meeting with Ms. Jacobs.
3. A: Was Mr. Cotter writing police reports at 10:30?
   B: No, he wasn't.
4. A: What kind of reports was he writing?
   B: He was writing financial reports.
5. A: What was he doing at 11:30?
   B: He was answering correspondence.
6. A: Was he having lunch at 12:00?
   B: Yes, he was.
7. A: Who was eating lunch with him?
   B: Mr. Webb was eating lunch with him.
8. A: Where were they having lunch?
   B: They were having lunch at Sol's Cafe.
9. A: Who was he talking to at 3:30?
   B: He was talking to Alan.
10. A: What were they discussing?
    B: They were discussing the budget.

3

2. was crossing	19. got
3. was speeding	20. was lying
4. didn't stop	21. was bleeding
5. was	22. was
6. saw	23. were questioning
7. was walking	24. said
8. saw	25. was crossing
9. noticed	26. went
10. was going	27. knocked
11. reached	28. happened
12. went	29. had
13. hit	30. was crossing
14. took out	31. didn't see
15. called	32. broke
16. didn't stop	33. had
17. happened	34. were not
18. came	

4

2. What did you do when you heard the noise?
3. What did you see when you looked in the direction of the sound?
4. Where were you standing when you saw the Honda?
5. Did the driver stop when the accident occurred?
6. What happened next?
7. Did you get a look at the driver while he was driving away?
8. What was the victim doing when the car hit her?

UNIT 5 (pages 24–26)

1

2. People used to read
3. People used to cook
4. People used to wash
5. People used to use
6. It used to take

2

2. didn't use to work
3. didn't use to have
4. used to take
5. didn't use to be
6. used to live
7. didn't use to like
8. didn't use to know
9. used to return
10. used to make

3

2. A: Where did she use to live?
   B: She used to live in New York.
3. A: Did she use to live in a house?
   B: No, she didn't.
4. A: What did she use to do?
   B: She used to be a student.
5. A: Which school did she use to attend?
   B: She used to attend City College.
6. A: Did she use to have long hair?
   B: Yes, she did.
7. A: Did she use to wear glasses?
   B: No, she didn't.
8. A: Did she use to be married?
   B: Yes, she did.

4

Today I ran into an old classmate. We used to be in the same science class. In fact, we used to ~~studied~~ *study* together for tests. He was a very good student, and he always ~~uses~~ *used* to get A's. At first I almost didn't recognize Jason! He looked so different. He used to ~~had~~ *have* very dark hair. Now he's almost all gray. He also used to ~~being~~ *be* a little heavy. Now he's quite thin. And he was wearing a suit and tie! I couldn't believe it. He never ~~use~~ *used* to dress that way. He only used to ~~wore~~ *wear* jeans! His personality seemed different, too. He didn't ~~used~~ *use* to talk very much. Now he seems very outgoing. I wonder what he thought of me! I'm sure I look and act different from the way I ~~was~~ used to too!

5

Answers will vary.

UNIT 6 (pages 27–34)

1

2. She's going to wash the car.
3. They're going to get gas.
4. She's going to make a left turn.
5. She's going to get a ticket.
6. They're going to crash.
7. They're going to eat lunch.
8. It's going to rain.

2

2. How long are you going to stay?
3. Are you going to stay at a hotel?
4. What are you going to do in San Francisco?
5. Are you going to visit Fisherman's Wharf?
6. Is your daughter going to go with you?
7. What is he going to do?
8. When are you going to leave?

3

2. He isn't going to take the train.
   He's going to fly OR take a plane.
3. He isn't going to travel alone.
   He's going to travel with his wife.
4. They aren't going to leave from Chicago.
   They're going to leave from New York City.
5. They aren't going to fly US Airways.
   They're going to fly FairAir.
6. They aren't going to leave on July 11.
   They're going to leave on June 11.
7. They aren't going to take Flight 149.
   They're going to take Flight 194.
8. It isn't going to depart at 7:00 A.M.
   It's going to depart at 7:00 P.M.
9. They aren't going to sit apart.
   They're going to sit together.
10. She isn't going to sit in Seat 15B.
    She's going to sit in Seat 15C.

4

2. will become
3. Will . . . replace
4. won't replace
5. will . . . operate
6. will . . . do
7. 'll be
8. 'll sing
9. 'll dance
10. Will . . . tell
11. will
12. won't . . . be
13. will . . . do
14. Will . . . have
15. will
16. will . . . help
17. 'll replace
18. 'll perform
19. won't be
20. will improve
21. will lose
22. will create
23. Will . . . need
24. will . . . look
25. won't look
26. 'll resemble
27. will . . . happen
28. 'll happen

5

Next Wednesday <u>is</u> the first performance of *Robots*. Melissa Robins <u>is playing</u> the leading role. Robins, who lives in Italy and who is vacationing in Greece, is not available for an interview at this time. She <u>is</u>, however, <u>appearing</u> on Channel 8's "Theater Talk" sometime next month.

Although shows traditionally begin at 8:00 P.M., *Robots*, because of its length, <u>starts</u> half an hour earlier.

Immediately following the opening-night performance, the company <u>is having</u> a reception in the theater lounge. Tickets are still available. Call 555-6310 for more information.

6

2. I'm going to do
3. I'll ask
4. it's going to rain
5. They're showing
6. we're going to have
7. it's going to spill, I'll be
8. I'll take
9. We're going to arrive
10. are we going to get
11. We'll take, will still be
12. We're landing
13. are you going to stay
14. we'll see

7

I'm going
~~I going~~ to stay here for a week with my parents.

We have a lot of fun things planned.
we're seeing OR *we're going to see*
Tomorrow night ~~we'll see~~ a play called *Robots*. Mom already bought the tickets for it. The play
we're having OR *we're going to have*
begins at 7:30, and before that ~~we have~~ dinner on Fisherman's Wharf. Right now we're sitting in Golden Gate Park, but we have to leave. The sky
's going to
is getting very dark. It ~~will~~ rain!
'll call
I ~~call~~ you soon.

8

Answers will vary.

UNIT 7 (pages 35–38)

1

2. gets up . . . 'll take (i)
3. is . . . 'll drink (c)
4. eat . . . 'll read (j)
5. finish . . . 'll do (g)
6. washes . . . 'll dry (e)
7. get in . . . 'll fasten (d)
8. gets . . . 'll drive (b)
9. stops . . . 'll need (f)
10. is . . . 'll be (a)

2

2. will apply (OR 's going to apply) . . . before . . . finishes
3. After . . . finishes . . . 'll visit (OR 's going to visit)
4. While . . . works . . . 'll take (OR 's going to take)
5. 'll visit (OR 's going to visit) . . . before . . . gets
6. When . . . finishes . . . 'll fly (OR 's going to fly)
7. 'll get married (OR 's going to get married) . . . when . . . 's
8. 'll return (OR 's going to return) . . . after . . . gets married
9. 'll move (OR 's going to move) . . . when . . . returns
10. After . . . moves . . . 'll look for (OR 's going to look for)

3

2. Vera saves enough money from her job, she's going to buy a plane ticket.
3. Vera goes home, she's going to buy presents for her family.
4. Vera arrives at the airport, her father will be there to drive her home.
5. Vera and her father get home, they'll have dinner.
6. Vera will give her family the presents . . . they finish dinner.
7. Vera's brother will wash the dishes . . . Vera's sister dries them.
8. The whole family will stay up talking . . . the clock strikes midnight.
9. they go to bed, they'll all feel very tired.
10. Vera will fall asleep . . . her head hits the pillow.
11. Vera wakes up the next morning, she'll call her friends.
12. She'll see her friends . . . she has breakfast.

4

I'm really looking forward to your arrival tomorrow. Before you ~~will~~ know it, you'll be here! After I ~~will~~ pick you up at the airport, we'll go straight to my parents' house. My mother is going to make a special dinner, but before we have

will go
dinner, you and I ~~go~~ for a drive with Paulo. Rio is a beautiful city, and we can't wait to show you some of the sights. After we ~~will~~ have dinner, some
^
of our friends will come over to meet you.

Let's talk on the phone once more, before
you leave
~~you're going to leave~~. I'm going out for a few
I'll call
hours, but ~~I call~~ you as soon as I get back. I'll speak to you soon.

5

Answers will vary.

UNIT 8 (pages 39–45)

1

2. Whose phone rang at midnight?
3. Who was calling for Michelle?
4. Who was having a party?
5. How many people left the party?
6. What surprised them?
7. Whose friend called the police?
8. How many police arrived?
9. What happened next?
10. Who told the police about a theft?
11. Whose jewelry disappeared?
12. How many necklaces vanished?

2

2. How many rooms does her apartment have? (f)
3. How much rent does she pay? (j)
4. When does she pay the rent? (c)
5. Who does she live with? (h)
6. What does she do? (g)
7. Which company does she work for? (d)
8. How long does she plan to stay there? (a)
9. How does she get to work? (b)
10. Why does she take the bus? (i)

3

2. Why did you leave Chicago?
3. Who moved with you?
4. Where did you get a job?
5. When did it start?
6. How many rooms does it have?

7. How many of the rooms came with carpeting?
8. How much do you each pay?
9. What do you need to buy?
10. Whose brother wants to visit her?
11. Who called last Sunday?
12. Who did you speak to?
13. When do they want to visit you?
14. Why is there plenty of room?

4

Answers will vary.

UNIT 9 (pages 43–45)

1

2. himself
3. themselves
4. itself
5. herself
6. yourself, yourselves OR yourselves, yourself
7. themselves
8. itself
9. themselves
10. ourselves

2

2. each other
3. herself
4. themselves
5. each other's
6. herself
7. yourselves
8. itself
9. ourselves
10. each other

3

2. are criticizing each other OR one another
3. is going to help himself
4. are talking to themselves
5. are introducing themselves OR one another
6. are talking to each other
7. drove herself
8. blames OR is blaming himself
9. are enjoying each other's OR one another's
10. are thanking each other OR one another

4

myself
I really enjoyed ~~me~~ at Gina's party! Hank was
each other OR one another
there and we talked to ~~ourselves~~ quite a bit. He's a little depressed about losing his job. The job
itself
~~himself~~ wasn't that great, but he needs the money. He's disappointed in himself. He thinks it's all his
himself
own fault, and he blames ~~him~~ for the whole thing.
me
Hank introduced ~~myself~~ to several of his friends. I

spoke a lot to this one woman, Cara. We have a lot of things in common, and after just an hour, we felt like we had known ~~each other's~~ *each other* forever. Cara, ~~himself~~ *herself*, is a computer programmer, just like me.

At first I was nervous about going to the party alone. I sometimes feel a little uncomfortable when I'm in a social situation by ~~oneself~~ *myself*. But this time was different. Before I went, I kept telling myself to relax. My roommate, too, kept telling ~~myself~~ *me*, "Don't be so hard on ~~you~~ *yourself*! Just have fun!" That's what I advised Hank to do too. Before we left the party, Hank and I promised ~~us~~ *each other* OR *one another* to keep in touch. I hope to see him again soon.

UNIT 10 (pages 46–50)

1

2. out	**11.** out
3. on	**12.** up
4. off	**13.** out
5. back	**14.** in
6. out	**15.** out
7. down	**16.** back
8. out	**17.** together
9. up	**18.** over
10. up	

2

2. Pick out, help . . . out	**6.** Look . . . over
3. look up	**7.** Do . . . over
4. Set up, talk over	**8.** Hand . . . in
5. Write up	

3

2. clean it up	**6.** turn it down
3. call her back	**7.** hand them in
4. turn it down	**8.** drop it off
5. wake him up	

4

2. Point out common mistakes. OR Point common mistakes out.
3. Talk them over.
4. Pick out a new problem. OR Pick a new problem out.
5. Work it out with the class.
6. Write the results up. OR Write up the results.
7. Go on to the next unit.
8. Make up the final exam questions. OR Make the final exam questions up.
9. Hand them out.
10. Set up study groups. OR Set study groups up.
11. Help them out.
12. Call off Friday's class. OR Call Friday's class off.

5

How are things going? I'm already into the second month of the spring semester, and I've got a lot of work to do. For science class, I have to write a term paper. The professor made ~~over~~ *up* a list of possible topics. After looking ~~over them~~ *them over*, I think I've picked one out. I'm going to write about chimpanzees. I've already looked *up* some information about them online ~~X~~^ . I found ~~up~~ *out* some very interesting facts.

Did you know that their hands look very much like their feet, and that they have fingernails and toenails? Their thumbs and big toes are "opposable." This makes it easy for them to pick things ~~out~~ *up* with both their fingers and toes. Their arms are longer than their legs. This helps ~~out them~~ *them out*, too, because they can reach out to fruit growing on thin branches that would not otherwise support their weight. Adult males weigh between 90 and 115 pounds, and they are about four feet high when they stand ~~out~~ *up*.

Like humans, chimpanzees are very social. They travel in groups called "communities." Mothers bring ~~out~~ *up* their chimps, who stay with them until about the age of seven. Even after the chimps grow up, there is still a lot of contact with other chimpanzees.

I could go on, but I need to stop writing now so I can clean ~~out~~ *up* my room (it's a mess!) a little before going to bed. It's late already, and I have to get ~~early up~~ *up early* tomorrow morning for my 9:00 class.

Please let me know how you are. Or call me. I'm often out, but if you leave a message, I'll call ~~back you~~ *you back* as soon as I can. It would be great to speak to you.

UNIT 11 (pages 51–58)

1

3. can read an English newspaper . . . could (read one)
4. couldn't read an English novel . . . can't (read one)

5. can speak on the phone . . . couldn't (speak on the phone)
6. couldn't speak with a group of people . . . can (speak with a group of people)
7. could write an e-mail . . . can (write one)
8. Before the course, he couldn't write a business letter, and he still can't (write one).
9. Now he can order a meal in English, and he could (order a meal in English) before too.
10. Now he can go shopping, and he could (go shopping) before too.

SUMMARY: can . . . could

2

2. A: What languages can you speak?
3. A: Could you speak Spanish when you were a child?
   B: No, I couldn't.
4. A: Could you speak French?
   B: Yes, I could.
5. A: Before you came here, could you understand spoken English?
   B: No, I couldn't.
6. A: Can you understand song lyrics?
   B: Yes, I can.
7. A: Before this course, could you write a business letter in English?
   B: No, I couldn't.
8. A: Could you drive a car before you came here?
   B: No, I couldn't.
9. A: Can you drive a car now?
   B: No, I can't.
10. A: Can you swim?
    B: Yes, I can.
11. A: Could you surf before you came here?
    B: No, I couldn't.
12. A: What can you do now that you couldn't do before?
    B: can do . . . couldn't do

3

2. are able to interpret
3. are not able to distinguish
4. are not able to understand
5. are able to hear
6. are able to get back
7. are able to read
8. is not able to recognize
9. is not able to work
10. are able to communicate

4

3. How will . . . be able to see
4. Will . . . be able to hear

5. No, you won't.
6. How will . . . be able to solve
7. Will . . . be able to enjoy
8. Yes, you will.

5

2. could read
3. could not OR couldn't accept
4. was able to accept
5. could see
6. will . . . be able to do
7. can do
8. can do
9. can speak
10. was able to achieve
11. will be able to get
12. can read
13. can change
14. can do

6

 Before I came to this country, I ~~can't~~ *couldn't* do many things in English. For example, I couldn't follow a conversation if many people were talking at the same time. I remember a party I went to. Everyone was speaking English, and I wasn't able *to* understand a word! I felt so uncomfortable. Finally, my aunt came to pick me up, and I ~~could~~ *was able to* leave the party.

 Today I can ~~be~~ understand much better. I am taking classes at the adult center. My teacher is very good. She can ~~explains~~ *explain* things well, and she always gives us the chance to talk a lot in class. When I finish this class, I ~~can~~ *will be able to* speak and understand a lot better.

 ~~Be~~ *Being* able to speak English well is very important to me. I practice a lot at home too. When I first came to this country, I ~~can't~~ *couldn't OR wasn't able to* understand very much TV, but now I can ~~be~~ understand much better. In fact, I can do a lot now, and I think in a few more months I ~~can~~ *'ll be able to* do even more.

7

Answers will vary.

UNIT 12 (pages 59–62)

1

2. c		**6.** a	
3. b		**7.** e	
4. h		**8.** g	
5. f			

2

2. we (please) review Unit 6? OR we review Unit 6, please?

3. I (please) borrow your pen? OR I borrow your pen, please?

4. I look at your (class) notes?

5. I come late to the next class?

6. my roommate (please) come to the next class with me? OR my roommate come to the next class with me, please?

7. I (please) ask a question? OR I ask a question, please?

8. we (please) use a dictionary? OR we use a dictionary, please?

9. we (please) leave five minutes early? OR we leave five minutes early, please?

10. my sister goes on the class trip with the rest of the class?

3

Answers will vary.

4

2. can bring		**7.** may not pay	
3. can bring		**8.** may not purchase	
4. can't OR cannot drink		**9.** can't OR cannot get	
5. can pay		**10.** may swim	
6. can pay			

5

I've been sick for the past two days. That's why I missed the last test. May I ~~taking~~ *take* a make-up exam? **Yes. If you bring a doctor's note.**
If I can take the exam, may I use my calculator during the test?
No, you ~~mayn't~~ *may not*! I did not allow calculators during this test.

Could my roommate ~~comes~~ *come* to class and take notes for me on Thursday?
Yes, he ~~could~~ *can*.

Do you mind ~~when~~ *if* he records the class for me?
Not at all. It's fine for him to record the class.
One last thing—I know I missed some handouts.

May I ~~have please~~ *please have* copies of them?
Sure. I'll give them to your roommate on Thursday.
Thanks a lot.

UNIT 13 (pages 63–67)

1

2. a		**7.** b	
3. h		**8.** i	
4. g		**9.** f	
5. j		**10.** e	
6. c			

"Yes" responses: 2, 4, 5, 6, 7, 9, 10
"No" responses: 1, 3, 8
Negative = "OK": 5

2

2. opening the window
3. buy some stamps
4. pick up a sandwich
5. staying late tonight
6. keep the noise down
7. come to my office
8. get Frank's phone number
9. explaining this note to me
10. lend me $5.00

3

2. Would you mind working on Saturday?
3. Will you please help me? OR Will you help me, please?
4. Would you please explain this? OR Would you explain this, please?
5. Could you please drive me home? OR Could you drive me home, please?

4

(Note 3) Will you return please the stapler? → Will you please return the stapler? OR Will you return the stapler, please?

(Note 5) Would you mind leave → Would you mind leaving

(Note 6) Could you please remember to lock the door. → Could you please remember to lock the door?

(Note 7) Would you please to call Ms. Rivera before the end of the day? → Would you please call Ms. Rivera before the end of the day? OR Would you call Ms. Rivera before the end of the day, please?

(Note 8) Also, would you mind to e-mail Lisa Barker a copy? → Also, would you mind e-mailing Lisa Barker a copy?

5

Answers will vary.

UNIT 14 (pages 68–72)

1

2. You shouldn't shout into the phone.
3. You should speak in a quiet, normal voice.
4. You should leave the room to make a phone call.
5. You shouldn't discuss private issues in public places.
6. You shouldn't stand too close to other people when you are talking on the phone.
7. You should pay attention to other people on the street when you are walking and talking.
8. You shouldn't dial while you are driving. OR You should never dial while you are driving.

2

2. should call
3. 'd better not forget
4. a. ought to see
   b. 'd better buy
5. should try
6. a. ought to think
   b. should look into
7. a. shouldn't talk
   b. should be
8. 'd better not call
9. ought to have
10. should get
11. shouldn't talk
12. 'd better hang up

3

3. What should I wear?
4. Should I bring a gift?
5. No, you shouldn't.
6. Should I bring something to eat or drink?
7. You should bring something to drink.
8. When should I respond?
9. You should respond by May 15.
10. Should I call Aunt Rosa?
11. No, you shouldn't.
12. Who should I call?
13. You should call Amy and leave a message at 555-3234.

4

Party Etiquette Quiz
Do you know what you should do at a party?
Check the best answer.

1. You are at a party and you can't remember someone's name. What ~~you should~~ *should you* do?
   ☐ a. You should ~~no~~ *not* ask the person's name.
   ☐ b. ~~You better~~ *You'd better* leave immediately!
   ☐ c. You ought *to* just ^ ask.

2. You don't know anyone at the party, and your host doesn't introduce you to the other guests. ~~Had you better~~ *Should you* introduce yourself?
   ☐ a. Yes, you should. You should say "Hi. My name's _____."
   ☐ b. No, you ~~should~~ *shouldn't*. You'd better tell the host to introduce you.

3. Your cell phone rings during the party. ~~You should~~ *Should you* answer it?
   ☐ a. Just let it ring. You ~~had not better~~ *'d better not* answer it.
   ☐ b. You should answer it, but just have a short conversation.
   ☐ c. You really ought to leave the room and speak to the person in private.

4. You had a very nice time at the party. How ~~you should~~ *should you* thank your host?
   ☐ a. You should just say "thank you" when you leave.
   ☐ b. You should send a "thank you" e-mail the next day.
   ☐ c. You ~~oughta~~ *ought to* write a long "thank you" letter and send a gift too.

5

Answers will vary.

UNIT 15 (pages 73–76)

1

2. a
3. b
4. g
5. j
6. e
7. i
8. f
9. d
10. h

2

2. Maybe you could / .
3. Let's / .
4. How about / ?
5. Why don't you / ?
6. Let's / .
7. Maybe we could / .
8. Why doesn't she / ?
9. Why don't you / ?
10. How about / ?
11. Maybe we could / .
12. That's a good idea / .

3

2. take the "T"
3. go to Haymarket
4. taking an elevator to the top of the John Hancock Observatory
5. take a boat excursion
6. going to the New England Aquarium
7. eat at Legal Sea Foods
8. walk along the waterfront
9. going shopping in Downtown Crossing
10. walk the Freedom Trail

4

Answers will vary.

UNIT 16 (pages 77–80)

1

2. brought
3. come
4. eaten
5. fallen
6. gotten
7. had
8. looked
9. lost
10. played
11. watched
12. won

2

2. since
3. since
4. for
5. Since
6. For
7. for
8. since

3

Biography A
2. since
3. Since
4. has gone on
5. For
6. have seen
7. Since
8. has earned
9. (has) broken

Biography B
1. has been
2. for
3. Since
4. has won
5. has become
6. has dreamed OR has dreamt
7. since
8. Since
9. has continued

4

2. A: How long has he been a professional golfer?
   B: (He's been a professional golfer) since he was 16. OR for _____ years.
3. A: Has he won any major tournaments since he turned professional?
   B: Yes, he has.
4. A: How long has he been in TV commercials?
   B: (He has been in TV commercials) for the past few years.
5. A: How long has Michelle Kwan been a skater?
   B: (She has been a skater) since she was five. OR for more than twenty years.
6. A: How many World Competitions has she won since 1986?
   B: She has won five.
7. A: Has she gotten an Olympic gold medal since she began competing?
   B: No, she hasn't.
8. A: Has she skated again since the Olympics?
   B: Yes, she has.

5

3. Min Ho has won three awards
4. Marilyn has entered two competitions
5. Victor and Marilyn haven't seen each other since 1998.
6. Karl has been a golfer since 1999.
7. Karl has lost three tournaments
8. Andreas hasn't been to (OR gone to) a tennis match

UNIT 17 (pages 81–84)

1

2. become
3. danced
4. drunk
5. fought
6. given
7. held
8. kept
9. known
10. sung
11. smiled
12. traveled

2

2. 've already looked
3. haven't found . . . yet
4. 've already seen
5. haven't gone . . . yet
6. 've already wasted
7. Have . . . decided . . . yet
8. haven't made up . . . yet

3

3. Has she bought two bookcases yet? Yes, she's already bought two bookcases.
4. Has she thrown away old magazines yet? No, she hasn't thrown away old magazines yet. OR No, she hasn't yet thrown away old magazines.
5. Has she found a painter yet? No, she hasn't found a painter yet. OR No, she hasn't yet found a painter.
6. Has she collected boxes for packing yet? Yes, she's already collected boxes for packing.
7. Has she bought a new couch yet? No, she hasn't bought a new couch yet. OR No, she hasn't yet bought a new couch.
8. Has she given away the old couch yet? Yes, she's already given away the old couch.
9. Has she cleaned the refrigerator and stove yet? No, she hasn't cleaned the refrigerator and stove yet. OR No, she hasn't yet cleaned the refrigerator and stove.
10. Has she made a list of cleaning supplies yet? Yes, she's already made a list of cleaning supplies.
11. Has she gotten a change-of-address form from the post office yet? Yes, she's already gotten a change-of-address form from the post office.
12. Has she invited the neighbors over for a goodbye party yet? No, she hasn't invited the neighbors over for a goodbye party yet. OR No, she hasn't yet invited the neighbors over for a goodbye party.

4

I'm writing to you from our new apartment!

We've already ~~be~~ *been* here two weeks, and we feel very much at home. But there's still a lot to do. Believe it or not, we haven't unpacked all the boxes ~~already~~ *yet*! We took most of our old furniture, so we don't need to get too much new stuff. We had to buy a new couch for the living room, but they haven't delivered it yet.

We've already ~~meet~~ *met* some of our new neighbors. They seem very nice. One of them ~~have~~ *has* already invited us over for coffee.

~~Had~~ *Have* you made vacation plans yet? As soon as we get the couch (it's a sleeper), we'd love for you to visit. ~~Already we've planned~~ *We've already planned* places to take you when you come!

UNIT 18 (pages 85–88)

1

2. decided	8. ridden
3. flown	9. seen
4. gone	10. swum
5. heard	11. traveled
6. kept	12. worked
7. made	

2

2. 've ridden
3. 've heard
4. 've seen
5. 's flown
6. 've swum
7. has decided
8. 's worked

3

2. have appeared
3. have . . . loved
4. have not stopped
5. has written
6. (has) contributed
7. have . . . received
8. has described
9. has introduced
10. has included
11. has given
12. has not been
13. has been
14. have done
15. have produced
16. has . . . encouraged
17. haven't read

4

2. How many times have you visited, I've visited Europe more than 10 times.
3. Have you ever been, I've recently been on an African safari.
4. Have you ever been, Yes, I've been to Costa Rica.
5. How often have you been, I've been there once.
6. Have you (ever) traveled, I've never traveled in China.
7. Have you ever gone up, I've never gone up in a hot-air balloon.
8. Have you ever swum, I've swum with dolphins many times.
9. Have you ever taken, I've never taken a group tour.

5

Answers will vary.

UNIT 19 (pages 89–93)

1

3. Tom has gone
4. Tom got
5. Tom has made
6. Tom met
7. Tom has been
8. Tom looked
9. Tom bought
10. Tom has paid
11. Tom has read
12. Tom has taken
13. Tom has given
14. Tom felt

2

2. got
3. 've been
4. did . . . have
5. became
6. had
7. were
8. did . . . last
9. divorced
10. Did . . . have
11. didn't
12. 've remained
13. saw
14. have become
15. Has . . . remarried
16. hasn't
17. did . . . fail
18. got
19. didn't know
20. did . . . meet
21. were
22. did . . . move
23. 've lived

3

2. began
3. got
4. had
5. was
6. has risen
7. occurred
8. has created
9. started
10. had
11. were
12. has . . . increased
13. stayed
14. got
15. has changed
16. has reached

4

Last month, I ~~have met~~ *met* the most wonderful guy. His name is Roger, and he is a student in my night class. He ~~lived~~ *'s lived* here since 1992. Before that he lived in Detroit too, so we have a lot in common. Roger ~~has been~~ *was* married for five years but got divorced last April.

Roger and I ~~spent~~ *have spent* a lot of time together. Last week I saw him every night, and this week ~~we~~ *we've* already gotten together three times after class. Monday night we ~~have seen~~ *saw* a great movie. ~~Did you see~~ *Have you seen* The Purple Room? It's playing at all the theaters.

We've decided to take a trip back to Detroit in the summer. Maybe we can get together. It would be great to see you again. Please let me know if you'll be there.

P.S. Here's a photo of Roger that ~~I've taken~~ *I took* a few weeks ago.

5

Answers will vary.

UNIT 20 (pages 94–98)

1

2. She's been writing articles about elephants since last month OR for a month.
3. Amanda and Pete haven't been living in New York since a few years ago OR for a few years.
4. They've been living in London since 2004 OR for _____ years.
5. Pete hasn't been selling books since last year OR for a year.
6. Pete and Amanda have been thinking of opening their own business since last year OR for a year.
7. Pete has been studying economics since last month OR for a month OR since he went back to school (last month).
8. Amanda and Pete have been looking for a new apartment since a month ago OR for a month.

2

2. has been selling
3. has been fighting
4. have opened
5. has . . . done
6. has been
7. has been traveling
8. has received
9. has been working
10. has written
11. has . . . been combining
12. has changed

3

2. have . . . been
3. have . . . been doing
4. 've been reading
5. Have . . . read
6. 've seen
7. Have . . . bought
8. 've been using
9. has . . . opened
10. 've been opening

4

2. How long has she been a businesswoman?
3. How much money has her business made this year?
4. How long has she been traveling around the world?
5. How many countries has she visited?
6. Have her shops been opening in Asia? OR Have her shops opened in Asia?
7. How many copies of her book has she sold?
8. Has she written any books since *Business as Unusual*?
9. How many awards has she won?
10. What has she been working on these days?
11. How long have she and her husband lived in England? OR How long have she and her husband been living in England?

5

It's the second week of the fall semester.

been taking
I've ~~taken~~ a business course with Professor McCarthy.

been
For the past two weeks, we've studying people

become   ^
who have ~~been becoming~~ very successful in the world of business. As part of the course, we've been reading books by or about internationally famous businesspeople.

finished
For example, I've just ~~been finishing~~ a book by Bill Gates, the CEO of Microsoft, called *Business @ the Speed of Thought*. It was

been reading
fascinating. Since then, I've ~~read~~ *Business as Unusual* by Anita Roddick, the owner of The Body

read
Shop. I've only ~~been reading~~ about 50 pages of the the book so far, but it seems interesting.

've been buying OR *'ve bought*
Although I ~~bought~~ her products ever since one of her stores opened in my neighborhood, I really didn't know much about her.

UNIT 21   (pages 99–102)

1

Proper nouns: Chirac, December, Korean, Todd
Common count nouns: chair, class, country, cup, euro, garden, hamburger, month, pen, president, snowflake, story
Common non-count nouns: furniture, history, honesty, ink, money, news, oil, rice, snow, spaghetti, sugar, swimming, water

2

2. Potatoes are, Rice is
3. Potato chips are, Americans eat . . . people
4. kills
5. Popcorn is
6. Peanuts are not
7. Peanut butter has
8. history . . . is
9. Ice cream is, Vanilla and chocolate are

3

2. many (c)
3. much (b)
4. many (c)
5. much (b)
6. many (b)
7. much (b)
8. many (a)

4

1. b. many
   c. a few
2. a. a lot of
   b. some
   c. a little
   d. enough
3. a. many
   b. any
   c. several
   d. a lot of
4. a. enough
   b. little

5

Answers will vary.

UNIT 22   (pages 103–106)

1

1. the . . . the
2. the
3. the
4. the, the
5. a, The . . . the
6. the
7. Ø, Ø, the . . . Ø
8. the, a
9. an, a
10. Ø, Ø
11. some, a . . . the . . . the
12. the, a, The

2

2. a
3. the
4. A
5. a
6. —
7. —
8. a
9. —
10. The
11. —
12. a
13. The
14. the
15. the
16. the
17. the
18. the
19. an
20. —
21. a
22. —
23. the

3

2. a
3. a
4. the
5. the
6. the
7. the
8. the
9. the
10. The
11. the
12. a
13. the
14. the
15. an
16. the
17. the
18. The
19. a
20. the
21. the
22. the
23. The
24. the
25. the
26. —
27. the

4

2. a
3. the
4. a
5. a
6. a
7. —
8. —
9. the
10. The
11. a
12. —
13. —
14. —
15. —
16. A OR The
17. an
18. a
19. —
20. a OR the
21. —
22. the

UNIT 23 (pages 107–110)

1

2. nice
3. fast
4. well
5. dangerous
6. beautifully
7. hard
8. safely
9. occasional
10. happy
11. sudden
12. carefully
13. angrily
14. unfortunate
15. badly
16. thoughtful
17. hungry
18. extremely

2

2. Good news travels fast!
3. It has five large rooms,
4. it's in a very large building,
5. it's very sunny.
6. It's not too bad.
7. It seems pretty quiet.
8. the landlord speaks very loudly.
9. He doesn't hear well.
10. Was it a hard decision?
11. we had to decide quickly.
12. I have to leave now.
13. Good luck with your new apartment!

3

2. hard
3. well
4. nice
5. extremely
6. comfortable
7. cold
8. pretty
9. friendly
10. safe
11. really
12. important
13. late
14. completely
15. empty
16. good
17. easily
18. near
19. frequently
20. nice
21. convenient
22. wonderful
23. completely
24. new
25. really
26. happy
27. happy

4

2. disturbed
3. entertaining
4. disgusted
5. inspiring
6. paralyzed
7. moving
8. moved
9. frightening
10. disturbed
11. touching
12. astonishing
13. frightening
14. bored
15. disappointed
16. touching
17. exciting
18. entertaining
19. bored

UNIT 24 (pages 111–116)

1

2. worse
3. bigger
4. more careful
5. cheaper
6. more comfortable
7. more dangerous
8. more difficult
9. earlier
10. more expensive
11. farther OR further
12. better
13. hotter
14. longer
15. noisier
16. prettier
17. slower
18. more terrible
19. wetter
20. wider

2

2. not as large as
3. just as big as
4. just as expensive as
5. not as varied as
6. not as long as
7. not as convenient as
8. not as late as
9. not as nice as
10. just as good as
11. not as good as
12. just as clean as

3

2. earlier
3. more comfortable
4. healthier than
5. better than
6. more exciting
7. taller than
8. quieter (OR more quiet) than
9. worse
10. later than
11. faster
12. easier

4

2. Y . . . cheaper than . . . X
3. Y . . . larger than . . . X
4. X . . . smaller than . . . Y
5. Y . . . heavier than . . . X
6. X . . . lighter than . . . Y
7. X . . . more efficient than . . . Y
8. Y . . . more effective than . . . X
9. Y . . . faster than . . . X
10. X . . . slower than . . . Y
11. X . . . noisier than . . . Y
12. Y . . . quieter (OR more quiet) than . . . X
13. Y . . . better than . . . X
14. X . . . worse than . . . Y

5

2. cheaper and cheaper OR less and less expensive
3. better and better
4. bigger and bigger
5. more and more varied
6. more and more popular
7. less and less healthy
8. heavier and heavier

6

2. The fresher the ingredients, the better the food.
3. The more popular the restaurant, the longer the lines.
4. The more enjoyable the meal, the more satisfied the customers.
5. The bigger the selection, the happier the customers.
6. The later in the day, the more tired the servers.
7. The more crowded the restaurant, the slower the service.
8. The better the service, the higher the tip.

7

Answers will vary.

UNIT 25 (pages 117–121)

1

2. the worst
3. the biggest
4. the cutest
5. the most dangerous
6. the most expensive
7. the farthest OR the furthest
8. the funniest
9. the best
10. the happiest OR the most happy
11. the hottest
12. the most important
13. the most intelligent
14. the most interesting
15. the lowest
16. the nicest
17. the noisiest
18. the most practical
19. the warmest
20. the most wonderful

2

2. Mexico City . . . the newest
3. New York City . . . the longest
4. Toronto . . . the shortest
5. The busiest . . . Mexico City
6. Toronto . . . the lowest
7. Toronto . . . the most expensive (OR Mexico City . . . the least expensive)
8. the cheapest . . . Mexico City

3

2. the least comfortable
3. the newest
4. the most beautiful
5. the easiest
6. the biggest
7. the fastest
8. the coolest
9. the hottest
10. the most convenient

11. the most interesting
12. the least dangerous
13. the most historic
14. the most crowded
15. The most efficient
16. the most dangerous
17. the least expensive
18. the quietest OR the most quiet

4

Greetings from Mexico City! With its
mixture of the old and the new, this is one of the
most interesting
~~interestingest~~ cities I've ever visited. The people are
friendliest OR *most friendly*
among the ~~friendlier~~ in the world, and they have
been very patient with my attempts to speak their
the
language. Spanish is definitely one of ~~a~~ most
beautiful languages, and I definitely want to take
hottest
lessons when I get home. This has been the ~~most hot~~
summer in years, and I'm looking forward to going
to the beach next week. The air pollution is also
worst
the ~~baddest~~ I've experienced, so I'll be glad to be
out of the city. By the way, we definitely did not
fastest   *most convenient*
need to rent a car. The ~~most fast~~ and ~~convenientest~~
way to get around is by subway.

5

Answers will vary.

UNIT 26 (pages 122–126)

1

2. more beautifully   the most beautifully
3. more carefully   the most carefully
4. more dangerously   the most dangerously
5. earlier   the earliest
6. farther OR further   the farthest OR the furthest
7. faster   the fastest
8. more quickly   the most quickly
9. sooner   the soonest
10. better   the best

2

2. ran as fast as
3. jumped as high as
4. didn't jump as high as
5. didn't throw the discus as far as
6. threw the discus as far as
7. didn't do as well as
8. didn't compete as successfully as

3

2. harder than
3. more slowly than OR slower than
4. faster
5. more accurately
6. more aggressively than
7. worse than
8. better
9. more successfully
10. more seriously
11. (more) regularly

Winning Team: George, Bob, Randy, Dennis
Losing Team: Alex, Rick, Larry, Elvin

4

2. E . . . the most slowly OR the slowest, more slowly OR slower than
3. higher than . . . B
4. E . . . the highest
5. farther than . . . E
6. E . . . the farthest
7. E . . . the best
8. E . . . the worst . . . better than

5

2. She's running more and more frequently.
3. He's throwing the ball farther and farther.
4. She's shooting more and more accurately.
5. He's jumping higher and higher.
6. He's running more and more slowly OR slower and slower.
7. They're skating more and more gracefully. OR They're scoring higher and higher.
8. They're practicing harder and harder.
9. He's driving more and more dangerously.
10. They're feeling worse and worse.

6

I just completed my run. I'm running much
than
longer ~~that~~ before.
Today I ran for 30 minutes without getting
more slowly OR *slower*
out of breath. I'm glad I decided to run ~~more slow~~.
farther
The more slowly I run, the ~~farthest~~ I can go.
I'm really seeing progress.
Because I'm enjoying it, I run more and more
frequently
~~frequent~~. And the more often I do it, the longer
and farther I can go. I really believe that running
quickly
helps me feel better more ~~quick~~ than other forms
of exercise. I'm even sleeping better than before!
I'm thinking about running in the next
as fast as OR *faster than*
marathon. I may not run ~~as fast than~~ younger

runners, but I think I can run ~~long~~ *longer* and farther. We'll see!

UNIT 27 (pages 127–130)

1

2. going
3. meeting
4. Sitting
5. running
6. lifting
7. doing
8. taking
9. Exercising
10. wasting

2

2. Dancing
3. lifting weights
4. walking (OR playing tennis) . . . playing tennis (OR walking)
5. swimming
6. lifting weights
7. walking (OR riding a bike) . . . riding a bike (OR walking)
8. Doing sit-ups
9. swimming
10. lifting weights (OR doing sit-ups), doing sit-ups (OR lifting weights)
11. running
12. playing tennis
13. Riding a bike
14. lifting weights

3

2. dislikes doing OR doesn't enjoy doing
3. enjoys dancing
4. mind teaching
5. kept practicing
6. denied (OR denies) stepping OR didn't admit (OR doesn't admit) stepping
7. considering taking
8. regrets not beginning
9. suggests going
10. admits feeling

4

Answers will vary.

UNIT 28 (pages 131–134)

1

2. of
3. to
4. of
5. to
6. about
7. in
8. on
9. to
10. in

2

2. succeeded in collecting
3. is worried about missing
4. are used to working
5. believe in talking
6. are tired of waiting
7. insists on reaching
8. approves of having
9. are opposed to going
10. looking forward to returning

3

2. striking
3. firing
4. permitting
5. being
6. getting
7. missing
8. trying
9. making
10. listening
11. seeing

4

Answers will vary.

UNIT 29 (pages 135–138)

1

2. want to see
3. refuses to go
4. threatened to end
5. hesitate (OR am hesitating) to take
6. seems to be
7. attempted to create
8. intend to stay
9. needs to speak
10. will agree to go

2

2. to do the dishes.
   him to do the dishes.
3. her to buy some milk.
   to buy some milk.
4. him to drive her to her aunt's.
   to drive her to her aunt's.
5. him to have dinner at her place Friday night.
   to have dinner at her place Friday night.
6. him to give her his answer tomorrow.
   to give her his answer tomorrow.
7. to cut his hair.
   her to cut his hair.
8. him to be home at 7:00.
   to get home at 8:00.
9. her to call him before she leaves the office.
   to call him before she left the office.
10. to see a movie Friday night.
    her to pick one out.

3

Annie answered my letter! She advised ~~we~~ *us* to go to counseling separately. I don't know if John will agree ~~going~~ *to go*, but I'm going to ask him to think about it. I attempted to introduce the topic last night, but he pretended ~~to not~~ *not to* hear me. I won't give up, though. I'm going to try to persuade ~~he~~ *him* to go. If he agrees to go, I may ask Annie ^*to* recommend some counselors in our area. I want ~~finding~~ *to find* someone really good. Our relationship deserves to have a chance, and I'm prepared ^*to* give it one. But I want John ~~feels~~ *to feel* the same way. I need to know that he's 100% committed to the relationship. I can be patient, but I can't afford ~~waiting~~ *to wait* forever.

4

Answers will vary.

UNIT 30 (pages 139–141)

1

3. He uses most of his salary (in order) to pay his college tuition.
4. He really wants an MP3 player (in order) to download music from the Internet.
5. He's going to wait for a sale in order not to pay the full price.
6. A lot of people came into the store today (in order) to look at the new gadgets.
7. They like talking to Ned (in order) to get information about the gadgets.
8. Someone bought an electronic navigator in order not to get lost.
9. Another person bought a tiny camcorder (in order) to bring it on vacation.
10. She used her credit card in order not to pay right away.
11. Ned showed her how to use the camcorder (in order) to do a lot of things.
12. She'll use it as a camera (in order) to take videos.

2

2. (in order) to return
3. in order not to pay
4. (in order) to carry
5. (in order) to sign
6. to have
7. (in order) to cut
8. (in order) to find out
9. in order not to miss
10. in order not to waste

3

I went to the store ~~for~~ *to* get some eggs and other things for dinner. I set the alarm on the electronic organizer to remind you to put the turkey in the oven. Could you call Cindi ~~too~~ *to* ask her to bring some dessert? Tell her she should come straight from school in order ~~to be not~~ *not to be* late. We'll eat at 6:00—if that's OK with you. Remember— you can use the organizer ~~for checking~~ *to check* the vegetable casserole recipe. I've got to run in order to get back in time to help you! Could I use your new camcorder ^*in* order to film the event?

UNIT 31 (pages 142–145)

1

2. The story is too long to fit on one page.
3. Ed Smith was nice enough to give us an interview.
4. These computers are getting too old for us to use.
5. The bookshelves aren't low enough for me to reach.
6. This newspaper has gotten good enough to win an award.
7. It's too noisy for me to concentrate.
8. The students are too busy to take a break.
9. Tina is good enough to work on a major newspaper.

Positive points: 3, 6, 9
Negative points: 2, 4, 5, 7, 8

2

2. late enough to call
3. too heavy for me to lift
4. too sweet to drink
5. small enough to fit
6. too noisy for me to think
7. too young to graduate
8. not hot enough to need
9. not sick enough to call
10. too high for me to reach
11. too tired to stay
12. good enough to go

3

I really think that people under 21 are too young ~~for driving~~ *to drive*. They are just not ~~enough~~ *experienced* ~~experienced~~ *enough* to operate a car. Driving is a risky activity, and the consequences are too important to ignore.

I totally agree that 13 is ~~to~~ *too* young to drive, but 21—come on, now! In my opinion, a 16-year-old is responsible enough ~~getting~~ *to get* behind the wheel of a car.

Everyone is talking about a MINIMUM age for driving. Well, what about a MAXIMUM? I think people over 75 are too old ~~too~~ *to* drive. Their physical reactions are just not ~~enough quick~~ *quick enough* anymore to drive.

Why don't they just require older people to take a road test every few years? The law requires us to test our <u>cars</u> every year. If it's important enough to check the car, it should be important enough ~~for~~ to check the driver! If you're good enough to pass the test, then you're good enough *to* ^drive. Period!

I don't think it's a question of too young or too old to drive. Younger people have a quicker reaction time, but older people have more experience. The important question is this: Is the person competent enough ~~being~~ *to be* on the road? Age alone just isn't that important.

4

Answers will vary.

UNIT 32 (pages 146–149)

1

2. living
3. Flying
4. to get
5. flying
6. to get over
7. doing
8. to do
9. to live
10. to do
11. seeing
12. to visit
13. getting

2

2. is tired of being
3. quit (OR stopped) drinking
4. believes in talking
5. forgot to bring
6. remember telling
7. stopped to get
8. afford to lose
9. refuses to live
10. intends to make
11. agreed to help
12. offered to drive

3

3. It's useful to work together.
4. Being careful is smart.
5. Being afraid all the time isn't good.
6. It isn't dangerous to fly.
7. It's a good idea to do relaxation exercises.
8. It's wonderful to travel.

4

Answers will vary.

UNIT 33 (pages 150–153)

1

2. listen to music than surf the net.
3. reading a book to hanging out with friends.
4. hanging out with friends to talking on the phone.
5. go to the movies than watch TV.
6. talk on the phone than listen to music.
7. going to the movies to playing computer games.
8. watching TV to listening to music.
9. read a book than watch TV.
10. reading a book to playing computer games.

2

2. He'd prefer (to have OR having) juice.
3. He'd rather have tomato juice than apple juice.
4. He'd rather not have a hot beverage.
5. He'd prefer not to have chicken soup.
6. He'd prefer a sandwich to cottage cheese and fruit.
7. He'd prefer a turkey sandwich to a tuna fish sandwich.
8. He'd rather have white bread.
9. He'd rather not have chocolate pudding.
10. He'd prefer vanilla ice cream to chocolate ice cream.

3

2. Do you prefer
3. Would you prefer
4. would you rather
5. Would (OR Do) you prefer
6. Would (OR Do) you prefer
7. Would (OR Do) you prefer
8. Do you prefer

4

Answers will vary.

UNIT 34 (pages 154–158)

1

2. must pass
3. must not forget
4. must obey
5. must stop
6. must not drive
7. must not change
8. must turn on
9. must not leave
10. must wear
11. must not talk
12. must sit
13. must . . . drink
14. must know

2

2. don't have to be
3. have to drive
4. doesn't have to drive
5. have to drive
6. don't have to wear
7. have to wear
8. have to have
9. don't have to have
10. have to keep
11. don't have to keep
12. have to wear

3

2. don't have to
3. don't have to
4. must not
5. don't have to
6. doesn't have to
7. must not
8. don't have to
9. don't have to
10. must not

4

2. A: Do . . . have to stop
   B: Yes, we do.
3. A: have . . . had to use
4. A: Did . . . have to work
   B: No, I didn't.
5. B: 'll have to get OR 'm going to have to get
6. B: had to drive
7. B: did . . . have to pay
8. A: Has . . . had to pay
   B: No, he hasn't.
9. A: Will (OR Do) . . . have to get
   OR Are . . . going to have to get
   B: Yes, I will. OR I do. OR I am.
10. B: has to have

5

2. b
3. b
4. c
5. a
6. b
7. a
8. b

6

Answers will vary.

UNIT 35 (pages 159–162)

1

2. is supposed to send
3. are supposed to provide
4. aren't supposed to provide
5. isn't supposed to pay for
6. is supposed to pay for
7. aren't supposed to pay for
8. is supposed to pay for
9. aren't supposed to give
10. are supposed to give
11. isn't supposed to supply
12. is supposed to pay for

2

2. Item 2. She was supposed to write the month first. OR She wasn't supposed to write the day first.
3. Item 4. She was supposed to print (OR write) her last name. OR She wasn't supposed to print (OR write) her first name.
4. Item 5. She was supposed to print (OR write) her first name. OR She wasn't supposed to print (OR write) her last name.
5. Item 6. She was supposed to write (OR include) her zip code.
6. Item 7. She was supposed to write (OR include) her state and (her) zip code.
7. Item 8. She was supposed to sign her name. OR She wasn't supposed to print her name.
8. Item 9. She was supposed to write the date.

3

1. is (OR was) supposed to land
2. are . . . supposed to get
3. Are . . . supposed to call
   Yes, we are.
4. are . . . supposed to tip
5. Is . . . supposed to be
   No, it isn't.
6. are . . . supposed to do
   're supposed to leave
7. Is . . . supposed to rain
   No, it isn't.
8. Are . . . supposed to shake

4

2. a. Adam wasn't going to get married.
   b. He was going to stay single.
3. a. Erica and Adam were going to get married in June.
   b. They weren't going to get married in September.
4. a. They weren't going to have a big wedding.
   b. They were going to have a small one.
5. a. They were going to live in Boston.
   b. They weren't going to move to Amherst.
6. a. Adam wasn't going to change jobs.
   b. He was going to keep his old one.

5

Answers will vary.

UNIT 36 (pages 163–166)

1

2. may go
3. could be
4. might be able to
5. might want
6. may not be

7. could go
8. might not understand
9. might not want
10. could stay
11. might be

2

2. might buy
3. is going to rain
4. is going to see
5. might go
6. is going to work

7. might have
8. is going to call
9. is going to read
10. might write

3

How are you? It's the Fourth of July, and it's raining really hard. They say it could clear up later.
Then again, it ~~could~~ *might OR may* not. You never know with the weather.

Do you remember my brother, Eric? He says hi. He might ~~has~~ *have* dinner with me on Saturday night. We may go to a new Mexican restaurant that just opened in the mall.

I definitely ~~might take~~ *am going to take* OR *am taking* some vacation time next month. Perhaps we could do something together. It might ~~not~~ be fun to do some traveling. What do you think? Let me know.

4

Answers will vary.

UNIT 37 (pages 167–172)

1

2. must not be
3. must feel
4. must not have
5. must know
6. must have
7. must not hear

8. must feel
9. must speak
10. must not study
11. must have
12. must not eat

2

1. might
2. must
3. must

4. might, could
5. could, must
6. must, couldn't

3

2. She must
3. They must
4. He must be
5. She might
   OR may
   OR could
6. It must be

7. They might be
   OR may be OR could
   be
8. She must
9. He might be OR may
   be OR could be
10. They must be

4

2. Could
3. can't
4. Bob
5. Chet
6. could

7. might
8. Dave
9. could
10. couldn't
11. Allen

5

Answers will vary.

6

Just got home. It's really cold outside. The temperature ~~could~~ *must* be below freezing because the walkway is all covered with ice. What a day! We went down to the police station to look at photos.
They must ~~having~~ *have* hundreds of photos. They kept showing us more and more. We kept looking, but it was difficult to be sure. After all, we only saw the burglar for a few seconds. They've ~~gotta~~ *got to* have other witnesses besides us! There were a lot of people at the mall that day. We ~~may not~~ *can't OR couldn't* be the only ones who got a look at the burglar! That's the one thing I'm certain of! In spite of our uncertainty with the photos, the detective was very patient. I guess he must be used to witnesses like us.
Nevertheless, it ~~have~~ *has* to be frustrating for him. I know the police ~~may~~ *must* really want to catch this guy.

Test: Units 1–8

PART ONE

Circle the letter of the correct answer to complete each sentence.

Example

Jason never _____ coffee.

A Ⓑ C D

(A) drink   (C) is drinking
(B) drinks   (D) was drinking

1. At the moment, Meng _____ on a report.

A B C D

(A) doesn't work   (C) work
(B) is working   (D) works

2. Water _____ at 100° C.

A B C D

(A) boil   (C) boils
(B) boiling   (D) is boiling

3. What _____ these days?

A B C D

(A) are you doing   (C) you are doing
(B) do you do   (D) you do

4. Do you have any aspirin? Ryan _____ a headache.

A B C D

(A) are having   (C) have
(B) has   (D) is having

5. Maria _____ to the park every day.

A B C D

(A) does   (C) goes
(B) go   (D) is going

6. When you get to the corner, _____ left.

A B C D

(A) is turning   (C) turning
(B) turn   (D) turns

7. Walk! _____ run!

A B C D

(A) Don't   (C) Not
(B) No   (D) You don't

8. Jennifer never _____ in the ocean.

A B C D

(A) is swimming   (C) swimming
(B) swim   (D) swims

(continued)

9. —Do you like spaghetti?
   —Yes, I _____.

   (A) am   **(C)** don't
   (B) do   **(D)** like

   A B C D

10. Tyler _____ me at 9:00 last night.

    (A) called   **(C)** is calling
    (B) calls   **(D)** was calling

    A B C D

11. There _____ a lot of people in the park yesterday.

    (A) are   **(C)** was
    (B) is   **(D)** were

    A B C D

12. One day last March, I _____ a very strange letter.

    (A) did get   **(C)** used to get
    (B) got   **(D)** was getting

    A B C D

13. Where _____ to school?

    (A) did you go **(C)** you go
    (B) you did go **(D)** you went

    A B C D

14. Claude didn't _____ in Canada.

    (A) lived   **(C)** used to live
    (B) use to live **(D)** used to living

    A B C D

15. Lauren left class early because she _____ a terrible headache.

    (A) had   **(C)** used to have
    (B) have   **(D)** was having

    A B C D

16. _____ is your English teacher?

    (A) Who   **(C)** Whose
    (B) Whom   **(D)** Why

    A B C D

17. Who _____ yesterday at the store?

    (A) did you see   **(C)** you saw
    (B) did you use to see **(D)** you were seeing

    A B C D

18. As soon as the light turned red, she _____ the car.

    (A) did stop   **(C)** stops
    (B) stopped   **(D)** was stopping

    A B C D

19. They _____ when the phone rang.

    (A) sleep   **(C)** was sleeping
    (B) slept   **(D)** were sleeping

    A B C D

20. Josh _____ the paper when I interrupted him.

  (A) read
  (B) reads
  (C) was reading
  (D) were reading

A B C D

21. —Who _____ there?
  —Mr. Jackson saw me.

  (A) did you see
  (B) saw you
  (C) you saw
  (D) you see

A B C D

22. —Whose teacher _____?
  —I called Kayla's teacher.

  (A) called you
  (B) did you call
  (C) you called
  (D) were calling

A B C D

23. It _____ tomorrow.

  (A) rains
  (B) rained
  (C) 's going to rain
  (D) 's raining

A B C D

24. Don't eat so much. You _____ sick later.

  (A) 're feeling
  (B) feel
  (C) felt
  (D) 'll feel

A B C D

25. The package will _____ tomorrow.

  (A) arrive
  (B) arrives
  (C) arriving
  (D) be going to arrive

A B C D

26. What _____ you do next month when you finish this course?

  (A) are
  (B) did
  (C) do
  (D) will

A B C D

27. Good night. I _____ tomorrow.

  (A) 'll see you
  (B) 'm going to see you
  (C) 'm seeing you
  (D) see

A B C D

28. Miguel and I _____ to the Crash concert. We already have our tickets.

  (A) are going
  (B) go
  (C) went
  (D) will go

A B C D

29. What will Michiko do when she _____ her license?

  (A) gets
  (B) is getting
  (C) is going to get
  (D) will get

A B C D

30. That driver _____ a speeding ticket. The police are right behind him.

  (A) gets
  (B) is getting
  (C) is going to get
  (D) will get

A B C D

(continued)

31. In the future, more cars _____ on electricity.

A B C D

    (**A**) are running   (**C**) run
    (**B**) ran   (**D**) will run

32. According to this schedule, the next train _____ in 10 minutes.

A B C D

    (**A**) leave   (**C**) left
    (**B**) leaves   (**D**) leaving

33. —Will you be home tomorrow night?
    —No, _____.

A B C D

    (**A**) I don't   (**C**) I will
    (**B**) I'm not   (**D**) I won't

34. I'll see you _____.

A B C D

    (**A**) at the moment   (**C**) last night
    (**B**) in an hour   (**D**) usually

35. —Why did you borrow those chairs from Andy?
    —I _____ a party next Saturday night.

A B C D

    (**A**) had   (**C**) 'm going to have
    (**B**) have   (**D**) 'll have

36. —Call me when you get home.
    —Don't worry. I _____.

A B C D

    (**A**) don't forget   (**C**) 'm not forgetting
    (**B**) forget   (**D**) won't forget

PART TWO

Each sentence has four underlined words or phrases. The four underlined parts of the sentence are marked A, B, C, and D. Circle the letter of the <u>one</u> underlined word or phrase that is NOT CORRECT.

Example
Ana <u>rarely</u> <u>is drinking</u> coffee, but <u>this morning</u> she <u>is having</u> a cup.
    A   B   C   D

A Ⓑ C D

37. Nicole <u>usually</u> <u>drives</u> to work, but <u>today</u> she <u>takes</u> the train.
    A   B   C   D

A B C D

38. Carlos <u>usually</u> doesn't <u>eat</u> pizza, but <u>at</u> the moment he <u>is wanting</u> a slice.
    A   B   C   D

A B C D

39. Frank <u>rarely</u> <u>goes</u> downtown because he <u>doesn't</u> <u>likes</u> the crowded streets.
    A   B   C   D

A B C D

40. Emily <u>usually</u> <u>is eating</u> in the cafeteria, but <u>these days</u> she <u>is eating</u> in the park.
    A   B   C   D

A B C D

41. <u>What</u> <u>you are</u> <u>studying</u> these days <u>at school</u>?
    A   B   C   D

A B C D

42. Rachel <u>don't</u> <u>speak</u> French, but <u>she's</u> <u>studying</u> Spanish at the Adult Center.
    A   B   C   D

A B C D

43. John <u>loves</u> tennis, but <u>rarely he</u> <u>plays</u> because he <u>doesn't have</u> time.
    A   B   C   D

A B C D

44. <u>Stand</u> up straight, <u>breathe</u> deeply, <u>hold</u> your head up, and <u>no look</u> down.
    A   B   C   D   **A B C D**

45. Megan <u>works always</u> late and <u>is</u> <u>rarely</u> home before 8:00 <u>at night</u>.
    A   B C   D   **A B C D**

46. I <u>know</u> you usually <u>don't wear</u> a jacket, but <u>wear</u> one today because it
   A   B   C   **A B C D**
<u>is feeling</u> cold outside.
 D

47. A breeze <u>is blowing</u>, the <u>sun</u> <u>shines</u>, and the sky <u>looks</u> clear and bright.
         A   B C   D   **A B C D**

48. Paulo <u>was</u> <u>drying</u> the dishes <u>when</u> he <u>was dropping</u> the plate.
      A   B   C   D   **A B C D**

49. When Anna <u>were</u> a little girl, she <u>used to</u> <u>pretend</u> that she <u>had</u> a horse.
        A   B   C   D   **A B C D**

50. What <u>did</u> you <u>used to</u> <u>do</u> when you <u>felt</u> afraid?
     A   B   C   D   **A B C D**

51. <u>As soon as</u> the alarm clock <u>rang</u>, she <u>woke up</u> and <u>was getting</u> out of bed.
  A   B   C   D   **A B C D**

52. Once <u>when</u> I <u>was</u> a little boy, I <u>used to get</u> sick and <u>went</u> to the hospital.
     A   B   C   D   **A B C D**

53. Who <u>you did</u> <u>see</u> when you <u>left</u> the building <u>last night</u>?
    A   B   C   D   **A B C D**

54. <u>While</u> I <u>drove</u> home, I <u>turned on</u> the radio and <u>heard</u> the news about
  A   B   C   D   **A B C D**
the accident.

55. When Marie <u>will get</u> <u>home</u>, she <u>is going to</u> <u>call</u> me.
       A   B   C   D   **A B C D**

56. <u>As soon as</u> she <u>finds</u> a new <u>job</u>, she <u>tells</u> her boss.
  A   B   C   D   **A B C D**

57. <u>I'll make</u> some sandwiches <u>before</u> <u>I'll leave</u> for the office <u>in the morning</u>.
  A   B   C   D   **A B C D**

58. According to the weather <u>forecast</u>, it <u>going to be</u> hot and sunny <u>tomorrow</u>
         A   B   C   **A B C D**
with a chance of a thunderstorm <u>in the afternoon</u>.
                    D

59. The doors <u>will</u> open until the train <u>comes</u> to a <u>complete</u> <u>stop</u>.
      A   B   C D   **A B C D**

60. My sister <u>is going to be</u> 16 <u>next</u> month, and she <u>has</u> a big party with all her
     A   B   C   D   **A B C D**
friends.

Test: Units 9–10

PART ONE

Circle the letter of the correct answer to complete each sentence.

Example
Jason never _____ coffee.   A Ⓑ C D

(A) drink   (C) is drinking
(B) drinks   (D) was drinking

1. Kayla lives by _____, but she's looking for a roommate.   A B C D

   (A) her   (C) himself
   (B) herself   (D) ourselves

2. People in my office exchange cards with _____ during the holidays. A B C D

   (A) myself   (C) ourselves
   (B) one another   (D) themselves

3. Thanks for offering to help, but I think I can do it _____.   A B C D

   (A) herself   (C) itself
   (B) himself   (D) myself

4. —Sara is talking to Austin.   A B C D
   —I didn't know that they knew _____.

   (A) each other   (C) them
   (B) others   (D) themselves

5. —Did you say something to me?   A B C D
   —No, I'm just talking to _____. I do that sometimes when I'm cooking.

   (A) me   (C) oneself
   (B) myself   (D) you

6. —There's soda in the refrigerator. Help _____.   A B C D
   —Thanks.

   (A) me   (C) you
   (B) myself   (D) yourself

7. —Where are your books?   A B C D
   —I put _____.

   (A) away   (C) them away
   (B) away them   (D) them off

8. It's an interesting story. Please _____.   A B C D

   (A) carry out   (C) hand in
   (B) go on   (D) write up

9. When Mei-Ling doesn't know a word, she always looks it _____   A B C D
   in the dictionary.

   (A) at   (C) over
   (B) into   (D) up

10. Please e-mail _____ when you get home.   A B C D

   (A) me   (C) you
   (B) myself   (D) yourself

11. It's my own fault. That's why I'm angry at _____.   A B C D

   (A) him   (C) me
   (B) himself   (D) myself

PART TWO

Each sentence has four underlined words or phrases. The four underlined parts of the sentence are marked A, B, C, and D. Circle the letter of the <u>one</u> underlined word or phrase that is NOT CORRECT.

Example
Ana <u>rarely</u> <u>is drinking</u> coffee, but <u>this morning</u> she <u>is having</u> a cup.   A Ⓑ C D
    A   B   C   D

12. Could we talk <u>over it</u> before you <u>turn</u> the whole <u>idea</u> <u>down</u>?   A B C D
              A   B   C D

13. Ethan <u>stood</u> <u>up</u> and introduced <u>himself</u> to <u>myself</u>.   A B C D
      A B   C   D

14. Marta <u>herself</u> <u>call</u> the meeting <u>off</u> <u>yesterday</u>.   A B C D
      A   B   C D

15. Do you want to get up <u>by yourself</u>, or would you like me to <u>wake</u> <u>up you</u>?   A B C D
                A   B   C   D

16. Don't <u>clean</u> <u>up</u> the kitchen by <u>itself</u>; I'd be glad to <u>help out</u>.   A B C D
        A   B   C   D

17. Rachel and Kevin know <u>themselves</u> well because <u>they</u> <u>grew</u> <u>up</u> together.   A B C D
                   A   B C D

18. Antonio and Monica always <u>look over</u> <u>each other</u> homework before they   A B C D
                    A   B

   <u>hand</u> <u>it in</u>.
    C   D

19. Before they <u>turned</u> <u>the music</u> <u>down</u>, I couldn't hear <u>me</u> think!   A B C D
          A   B   C   D

20. Tom asked <u>me</u> to <u>pick</u> some stamps for <u>him</u> at the post office <u>up</u>.   A B C D
         A   B   C   D

Test: Units 11–15

PART ONE

Circle the letter of the correct answer to complete each sentence.

Example
Jason never _____ coffee.

(A) drink   (C) is drinking
(B) drinks   (D) was drinking

A (B) C D

1. —Would you shut the door, please?
—_____

(A) Certainly.   (C) Yes, I could.
(B) No, I can't.   (D) Yes, I would.

A B C D

2. Why _____ a movie tonight?

(A) about seeing   (C) not seeing
(B) don't we see   (D) we don't see

A B C D

3. Courtney can't speak German yet, but after a few lessons she _____ speak a little.

(A) can   (C) is able to
(B) could   (D) will be able to

A B C D

4. In 2002, Canadian figure skaters Jamie Salé and David Pelletier _____ win the gold medal at the Winter Olympics.

(A) can   (C) was able to
(B) could   (D) were able to

A B C D

5. I _____ make new friends since I moved here.

(A) can't   (C) haven't been able to
(B) couldn't (D) 'm not able to

A B C D

6. She _____ better not arrive late.

(A) did   (C) had
(B) has   (D) would

A B C D

7. —Do you mind if I borrow a chair?
—_____ Do you need only one?

(A) I'm sorry.   (C) Yes, I do.
(B) Not at all.   (D) Yes, I would.

A B C D

8. Would you mind _____ me tomorrow?   A B C D

    (**A**) call   (**C**) to call
    (**B**) calling   (**D**) if you call

9. You _____ miss the deadline or you'll have to pay a late fee.   A B C D

    (**A**) better not   (**C**) 'd better not
    (**B**) 'd better   (**D**) had no better

10. _____ take the train instead of the bus? It's faster.   A B C D

    (**A**) How about   (**C**) Why don't
    (**B**) Let's   (**D**) Why not

11. May my sister _____ to class with me tomorrow?   A B C D

    (**A**) come   (**C**) coming
    (**B**) comes   (**D**) to come

12. **A:** Would you please explain that again?   A B C D
    B: Yes, _____.

    (**A**) certainly   (**C**) not at all
    (**B**) I would   (**D**) I do

PART TWO

Each sentence has four underlined words or phrases. The four underlined parts of the sentence are marked A, B, C, and D. Circle the letter of the <u>one</u> underlined word or phrase that is NOT CORRECT.

    Example
    Ana <u>rarely</u> <u>is drinking</u> coffee, but <u>this morning</u> she <u>is having</u> a cup.   A Ⓑ C D
          A   B   C   D

13. When <u>you will</u> <u>be</u> <u>able to</u> <u>tell</u> me your decision?   A B C D
          A   B   C   D

14. <u>Why don't</u> <u>we</u> <u>see</u> a movie Friday <u>night.</u>   A B C D
          A   B C   D

15. <u>Do</u> you <u>mind</u> <u>when</u> I postpone our Wednesday <u>appointment?</u>   A B C D
     A   B   C   D

16. <u>May</u> <u>he</u> <u>has</u> until <u>tomorrow</u> to hand in his paper?   A B C D
     A   B C   D

17. <u>Let's</u> <u>to leave</u> the party <u>early enough</u> <u>to catch</u> the last bus.   A B C D
     A   B   C   D

18. <u>Could</u> you <u>remember</u> <u>to bring</u> home <u>please</u> the newspaper?   A B C D
     A   B   C   D

19. You really ought <u>be</u> <u>more</u> <u>careful</u> or you <u>'ll get</u> into trouble.   A B C D
                 A   B C   D

20. <u>Would</u> you mind <u>to tell</u> me when you <u>are going to</u> <u>be</u> late?   A B C D
     A   B   C   D

Test: Units 16–20

PART ONE

Circle the letter of the correct answer to complete each sentence.

Example

Jason never _____ coffee.   A Ⓑ C D

(A) drink   (C) is drinking
(B) drinks   (D) was drinking

1. Samantha _____ in Mexico since 1991.   A B C D

   (A) is living   (C) have lived
   (B) has lived   (D) lived

2. John has already _____ this course.   A B C D

   (A) been taking   (C) takes
   (B) taken   (D) took

3. The journalist hasn't finished the article _____.   A B C D

   (A) already   (C) then
   (B) now   (D) yet

4. The department store has been in business _____ many years.   A B C D

   (A) already   (C) in
   (B) for   (D) since

5. How many cups of coffee have you _____ this morning?   A B C D

   (A) been drinking   (C) drink
   (B) drank   (D) drunk

6. Amanda _____ Texas six years ago.   A B C D

   (A) has been leaving (C) left
   (B) has left   (D) used to leave

7. They have been _____ lunch in the same cafeteria for 10 years. A B C D

   (A) ate   (C) eaten
   (B) eat   (D) eating

8. The Jordans _____ at R & J Corporation since 1999.   A B C D

   (A) are working   (C) have been working
   (B) has been working (D) worked

9. Have you read any good books _____?   A B C D

    (A) already   (C) lately
    (B) ever   (D) now

10. It _____ all day, so we haven't left the house.   A B C D

    (A) is raining   (C) rains
    (B) has been raining (D) rained

11. —Has the mail come yet?   A B C D
    —Yes, it _____.

    (A) did   (C) have
    (B) has   (D) is

12. I'm sorry I'm late. How long _____?   A B C D

    (A) did you wait   (C) have you waited
    (B) have you been waiting (D) you have been waiting

13. —What are you doing?   A B C D
    —I _____ on this report all morning.

    (A) work   (C) 've worked
    (B) 've been working (D) worked

14. _____ you cut your hair lately?   A B C D

    (A) Are   (C) Were
    (B) Did   (D) Have

PART TWO

Each sentence has four underlined words or phrases. The four underlined parts of the sentence are marked A, B, C, and D. Circle the letter of the <u>one</u> underlined word or phrase that is NOT CORRECT.

    Example
    Ana <u>rarely</u> <u>is drinking</u> coffee, but <u>this morning</u> she <u>is having</u> a cup.   A Ⓑ C D
          A   B   C   D

15. <u>When</u> she <u>was</u> a child, she <u>has worked</u> in a factory <u>for</u> more than three years.   A B C D
     A   B   C   D

16. Eric <u>have</u> <u>been sleeping</u> <u>for</u> more than <u>three hours</u>.   A B C D
       A   B   C   D

17. Last night we <u>have rented</u> two <u>DVDs</u> and <u>watched</u> them with some <u>friends</u>.   A B C D
           A   B   C   D

18. Jennifer <u>hasn't</u> <u>done</u> a thing <u>since</u> she <u>has gotten</u> to work.   A B C D
         A   B   C   D

19. <u>Since</u> I <u>have known</u> Daniel, he <u>had</u> three different <u>jobs</u>.   A B C D
   A   B   C   D

20. She <u>hasn't</u> <u>washed</u> the dishes or <u>made</u> the beds <u>already</u>.   A B C D
     A   B   C   D

Answer Key for Tests

Note: Correct responses for Part Two questions appear in parentheses.

UNITS 1–8

Part One

1. B	10. A	19. D	28. A
2. C	11. D	20. C	29. A
3. A	12. B	21. B	30. C
4. B	13. A	22. B	31. D
5. C	14. B	23. C	32. B
6. B	15. A	24. D	33. D
7. A	16. A	25. A	34. B
8. D	17. A	26. D	35. C
9. B	18. B	27. A	36. D

Part Two

37. D (is taking OR is going to take)
38. D (wants)
39. D (like)
40. B (eats)
41. B (are you)
42. A (doesn't)
43. B (he rarely)
44. D (don't look)
45. A (always works)
46. D (feels)
47. C (is shining)
48. D (dropped)
49. A (was)
50. B (use to)
51. D (got)
52. C (got)
53. A (did you)
54. B (was driving)
55. A (gets)
56. D (will tell OR is going to tell)
57. C (I leave)
58. B (is going to be)
59. A (won't)
60. D (is going to have OR is having)

UNITS 9–10

Part One

1. B	4. A	7. C	10. A
2. B	5. B	8. B	11. D
3. D	6. D	9. D	

Part Two

12. A (it over)
13. D (me)
14. B (called)
15. D (you up)
16. C (yourself OR yourselves)
17. A (each other OR one another)
18. B (each other's)
19. D (myself)
20. D (pick up OR pick some stamps up)

UNITS 11–15

Part One

1. A	4. D	7. B	10. D
2. B	5. C	8. B	11. A
3. D	6. C	9. C	12. A

Part Two

13. A (will you)
14. D (?)
15. C (if)
16. C (have)
17. B (leave)
18. D (please *goes after* you, remember, *or* newspaper)
19. A (to be)
20. B (telling)

UNITS 16–20

Part One

1. B	5. D	9. C	13. B
2. B	6. C	10. B	14. D
3. D	7. D	11. B	
4. B	8. C	12. B	

Part Two

15. C (worked)	18. D (got)
16. A (has)	19. C (has had)
17. A (rented)	20. D (yet)

Notes

Notes

Notes